# THE HORSE LOVER'S MISCELLANY

# THE HORSE LOVER'S MISCELLANY

## Wit, Wisdom and Wonders

J. C. Jeremy Hobson

Quiller

Copyright © 2025 J. C. Jeremy Hobson

First published in the UK in 2025
by Quiller, an imprint of Amberley Publishing Ltd

British Library Cataloguing-in-Publication Data
A catalogue record for this book is available
from the British Library

ISBN 978-1-84689-410-7 (hardback)
ISBN 978-1-84689-411-4 (e-book)

The right of J. C. Jeremy Hobson to be identified as the author of this work has been asserted in accordance with the Copyright, Design and Patent Act 1988. The information in this book is true and complete to the best of our knowledge. All recommendations are made without any guarantee on the part of the Publisher, who also disclaims any liability incurred in connection with the use of this data or specific details.

All rights reserved. No part of this book may be reproduced or transmitted in any form or by any means, electronic or mechanical including photocopying, recording or by any information storage and retrieval system, without permission from the Publisher in writing.

Typesetting by SJmagic DESIGN SERVICES, India.
Printed in the UK

## Quiller
An imprint of Amberley Publishing Ltd
The Hill, Merrywalks, Stroud, GL5 4EP
Tel: 01453 847800
Email: info@quillerbooks.com
Website: www.quillerpublishing.com

Appointed GPSR EU Representative:
Easy Access System Europe Oü, 16879218
Address: Mustamäe tee 50, 10621, Tallinn, Estonia
Contact Details: gpsr.requests@easproject.com, +358 40 500 3575

# CONTENTS

| | | |
|---|---|---|
| Acknowledgements | | 7 |
| 1 | Starting from Scratch | 10 |
| 2 | A Little Bit of History | 14 |
| 3 | Fiction and Superstition | 23 |
| 4 | Famous Horses | 29 |
| 5 | Equine Epitaphs | 43 |
| 6 | Horses in War | 55 |
| 7 | Working Horses | 68 |
| 8 | Equine Artists | 83 |
| 9 | Horses on Screen | 94 |
| 10 | Stables and Stabling – The Grand and Not so Grand | 105 |
| 11 | Turf Talk | 116 |
| 12 | In Pursuit of the Uneatable | 127 |
| 13 | Getting into the Habit | 135 |
| 14 | One for the Road | 139 |
| 15 | At Your Service | 146 |

| | | |
|---|---|---|
| 16 | Transports of Delight | 154 |
| 17 | Show Time | 161 |
| 18 | A Clear Round | 171 |
| 19 | Dressage | 181 |
| 20 | Anyone for Polo? | 191 |
| 21 | All the Fun of the Fair | 201 |
| 22 | The Last Laugh – A Little Round-up of Horse-related Jokes | 210 |
| Bibliography, References and Sources | | 217 |

# ACKNOWLEDGEMENTS

In no particular order, a huge 'thank you' to each and all of the following: Nik Smith and Helen Safe for sharing their experience and general information about donkeys; to Liz Bennett and Liz Wright, editor of *The Country Smallholder* and of *The Donkey* (the annual magazine of the Donkey Breed Society) for specific detail and photographs regarding Jimmy the donkey. Gill Parker kindly gave permission to show our photograph of her sculpture *Brewers Horse* on display at Sculptures by the Lakes – as did Monique and Simon Gudgeon, owners of Sculptures by the Lakes. Nepotism notwithstanding, thank you to Melinda Hobson for her photographic contributions, my sister-in-law Mandy Shepherd for the image of her wonderful painting and to Melinda's cousin Paul Crago for sharing his knowledge of the showjumping world as well as information (and photographs) appertaining to his mother, Judy Crago.

I'm indebted to my long-time friend and hunting companion Alex Warne for the use of his evocative and emotive photographs of the horses and soldiers preparing for the First World War; to Matt Limb who was kind enough to provide the photograph of the two ponies up in the Highlands of Scotland and to Sarah Benwell for the extremely atmospheric one of the New Forest ponies at the Stanpit Marsh round-up. All do, I think, greatly enhance the pictorial element of the book and help explain some of the written content.

Others to thank for their interest in this project – and their willingness to facilitate photographs in whatever shape or form – are Jenny Hand, director of the Munnings Art Museum; Valérie Blanchet-Guillot; David Parks; Martin and Philippa Whitley; Rachel Green; Joanna Smith Hazel Mansell-Greenwood of Greenwood Studios, Kevin Madgewick (Madgewick Carriage Masters); Paulette and Alan Coe (Layer Marney Horse Drawn Carriages) and renowned sculptor Rupert Till. Thanks, too, to Elizabeth Fox-Andrews for giving up her time and facilitating a photo opportunity with polo ponies outwintered in her fields.

Thank you to Guy Simmonds for agreeing to my including his essay, 'Lost my Bottle'; to Jeremy Whaley for allowing me to incorporate his thoughts regarding the skills of a good farrier and to Dave Pike for giving permission to refer to www.beyondtheflamesandmore.home.blog concerning the fascinating history of the London fire horses.

In terms of copyright, very many grateful thanks to Pippa Roome, magazine editor of *Horse & Hound* for permission to quote from a 2022 article outlining the 'rags to riches' story of Red Rum; Richard Dodman, director of Fox Chapel Publishers International for permission to use the extract from *Hollywood Hoofbeats: The Fascinating Story of Horses in Movies and Television*, published by Companion House; Quiller Publishing for allowing extracts from Peter Holt's book *The Keen Foxhunter's Miscellany*; Nina Yakinya, rights assistant at Bonnier Books and to author Albert Jack for agreeing to my quoting from *Red Herrings and White Elephants*. Equal thanks must also go to Gemma Davis and Paula Lester at *Country Life* magazine

## Acknowledgements

for clearing content from *Curious Observations: A Country Miscellany*; to Jane Camillin of *Racing Post* Books for allowing 'fair use' of extracts from *Warrior: The Amazing Story of a Real War Horse*. Likewise, Rosaline Jackson-Keys of *Encyclopaedia Britannica*, Inc. regarding material concerning the history of 'Clever Hans'. Massive thanks also to the unknown authors and compilers of the many websites I've consulted to either verify facts or gain the most up-to-date information.

In compiling this book I have obviously drawn from various websites, books, newspaper cuttings and magazine articles. In accordance with my understanding of the UK's copyright laws, I have not necessarily sought permission to quote very minor extracts from such sources – but have, where appropriate, mentioned the origin within the text and would like to assure anyone concerned that I have not taken any quote and used it out of context ... or to the detriment of what was intended by the original author. However, should anyone feel that any references to a particular source or quote has not been duly or correctly acknowledged, I would be grateful if they got in touch with the publishers in order that any unintentional omissions can be rectified in future editions.

Of course, my most sincere and ardent thanks are due to Angeline Wilcox, my editor at Quiller Publishing – and to all those at Quiller Publishing responsible for commissioning *The Horse Lover's Miscellany*; editing and proofreading it, publicising it and getting it out into the big wide world. There's a great deal of behind-the-scenes work involved with book production and I'm extremely grateful to every member of the team.

Finally, a little disclaimer! In a compilation of this nature, some widely accepted research as recorded, may not be entirely accurate. As is the way of much information passed down through the years, stories get altered, become embellished, or even take on the persona of legend and folklore.

# I

# STARTING FROM SCRATCH

Appropriately enough when commencing a book of this nature, the phrase 'starting from scratch' (meaning to do something from the very beginning), comes from the way races were begun in the days before the introduction of starting stalls and the competitors were simply expected to line up behind a line that had been scratched in the turf.

There are many horse-related expressions: 'champing at the bit'; 'shutting the stable door after the horse has bolted'; 'he's a dark horse' ... the list is endless. Several words in common usage in the English language are horse-related, too. Any places of entertainment today known as the Hippodrome are likely to be home to the performing arts, pantomimes and casinos but, in times past, it was used specifically to describe venues for horse racing and/or other horse-related activities. The name is derived from 'hippos', used by the ancient Greeks to indicate the horse. 'Hippocampus' seemingly refers to a curious seahorse-like creature in Greek mythology and is nowadays used to name a part of the brain due to the fact that it was thought to resemble this unusual aquatic creature. In Latin, *equus* is used to loosely describe a connection with the horse – from which come the words equine and equestrian.

*Starting from Scratch*

In poetry, the love of horses ranges from the humorous and light-hearted 'Hunter Trials' by John Betjeman to the sorrowful (and somewhat maudlin) verse 'A Soldier's Kiss' by First World War poet, Henry Chappell. One of Shakespeare's characters says of his mount: 'When I bestride him, I soar, I am a hawk. He trots the air, the earth sings when he touches it …' In Michael Morpurgo's *War Horse*, a soldier remarks of the equine hero: 'There's a nobility in his eye, a regal serenity about him. Does he not personify all that men try to be and never can be?'

Famously, the Emperor Caligula was supposed to have loved his horse Incitatus so much that he made it a member of the Roman senate and, in 2012, an owner in Stornoway, Scotland, began keeping her horse in the house after a dispute with neighbours.

William Cobbett (1763–1835) was the son of a farmer and an agricultural activist. Probably best known for his book *Rural Rides* (first published in 1830) he was not slow to appreciate the qualities of a good horse and in November 1821, describing a day out on an animal loaned to him by 'Messrs Palmer' at Ross-on-Wye, wrote:

> They put me upon a horse that seemed to have been made on purpose for me, strong, tall, gentle and bold; and that carried me either over or through everything. I, who am just the weight of a four-bushel [approximately 224 lb or 102 kg] sack of good wheat, actually sat on his back from daylight in the morning to dusk (about nine hours), without once setting foot on the ground.

It is also worth repeating this oft-used quote from Winston Churchill – a lifetime lover of horses and a keen, proficient horseman. He included it in his book, *My Early Life*, published in 1930:

> I say to parents, especially to wealthy parents, 'Don't give your son money. As far as you can afford it, give him horses.' No one ever

came to grief – except honourable grief – through riding horses. No hour of life is lost that is spent in the saddle. Young men have often been ruined through owning horses, or through backing horses, but never through riding them ...

Not always have horses been so well loved, well considered and well treated. Anna Sewell's book *Black Beauty* was written in part to highlight the cruelty some endured – often in the name of fashion such as when 'bearing reins' were used on carriage horses purely for the sake of appearance. In Chapter Ten ('A Talk in the Orchard'), the eponymous hero listens to another horse (Sir Oliver) telling of his experiences regarding the practice of tail docking which, as defined in Britain by the Docking and Nicking of Horses Act 1949, is '... the deliberate removal of any bone or any part of a bone from the tail ...'

> ... it was a cruel, shameful, cold-blooded act! When I was young I was taken to a place where these cruel things were done; I was tied up, and made fast so that I could not stir, and then they came and cut off my long and beautiful tail, through the flesh and through the bone, and took it away ... it was not only the pain, though that was terrible and lasted a long time; it was not only the indignity ... it was this, how could I ever brush the flies off my sides and my hind legs any more? You who have tails just whisk the flies off without thinking about it, and you can't tell what a torment it is to have them settle upon you and sting and sting, and have nothing in the world to lash them off with.

Training – more likely 'breaking' – horses was, for many years, associated with cruel practice. It is said, for instance, that in order to make horses go faster, a live hedgehog would be tied under their tails as an inducement while in other circumstances, the

*Starting from Scratch*

breaker would resort to twitches, rowelled bits, and unnecessarily sharp spurs in order to 'master' their horse.

Although undoubtedly cared for in the best manner possible given the circumstances, the atrocities endured by the horses and mules taken out to France during the First World War can hardly be imagined. Through a combination of exhaustion, starvation, drowning in a combination of mud and water, falling in shell holes, being shot and blown up, it's reckoned that some 8 million of them died as a result of human conflict on the Western Front.

Some of the horses 'called up' for war, came from the fields and pastures of Britain where they had been used to work the land; others had spent a working life in the towns and cities pulling brewery drays, delivery vans and omnibuses. Yet more (those taken with officers and cavalry riders in mind) were hunters, or used to pull the traps and gigs of rural gentry, or to provide quick and reliable transportation for the local doctor out on call – or even just for the simple pleasure of riding for its own sake.

In all aspects, the history and development of the horse from work-animal to companion is fascinating. While some people – such as English poet Walter Savage Landor (1775–1864), who once opined: 'Next to servants, horses are the greatest trouble in life' – might not have been their most ardent admirers, many more have discovered the pleasures to be had when spending time with any equine. Nineties rapper Vanilla Ice is a huge fan: 'I love horses, I love watching them. There's just something about horses, they are as tranquil as the ocean.' Whether oceans are ever tranquil is a moot point, but it is a fact that being around horses is undoubtedly good for mind, body and soul. It is perhaps just as well that horses cannot talk for there have been many untold secrets and confidences whispered in their ears which, in many instances, would not bear repeating!

# 2

# A LITTLE BIT OF HISTORY

Around 50 million years ago, a small animal around the size of a hare lived in swamps and it is thought to be an early ancestor of the horse. It had four toes on each of its front feet and three each on the back, each toe ending in a hoof. Known by scientists and biologists as either *Sifrhippus* or *Eohippus* (the latter moniker given to them by the American palaeontologist Othniel Charles Marsh), evidence of their evolutionary connection to the modern-day equine is thought to be found in the 'chestnut' – the small lumpy protuberance on the inside of the legs – and in the 'ergot', the little growth to be found on the back of the fetlock joints. These, it is said, are all that is left of the toes of the animal that lived all those millennia ago – and which would eventually become the horses, ponies and donkeys (and zebras!) that we know and love today.

## The north–south divide

Giving her take on the development of the horse over millennia, in 1944, Judith Blunt-Lytton, 16th Baroness Wentworth, was of the opinion that the original wild stock of the world could be divided into two distinct types:

### The Northern Type

The rock pictures of Southern Europe (possibly dating from 50,000 years ago show ... cold-blooded, heavy-boned, rather asinine horses ... with small angular sleepy eyes placed high in a convex skull with shallow jaw; they had much coarse hair, erect manes and low tail-carriage. This coarse-fibred, phlegmatic, thick-haired, thick-skinned ram-headed, slow breed with all its variations and its descendants can be classed as *Equus Frigidus*; and to it belong the prehistoric Great Horse of Europe, the big Battle Horse, our own Carthorse, the Mongolian and the Germanic horses of the smaller type, and some of the European ponies.

### The Southern Type

This hot-blooded, highly strung, light-limbed, concave-headed breed, with its derivations, is native to the warm sunny climates of the south and east. Only one example of this appears in European rock paintings in the form of a speckled pony; the pure Arabian only appears in the rock carvings of Arabia (where it is often depicted galloping with a rider carrying a spear) and of Egypt (1800 BC) where it is shown both ridden and driven. The Arabian horse, *Equus Arabicus*, is the root stock from which all the various Southern varieties are derived. It is the source of all pure breeding and the root stock also of the racing type being the earliest known racehorse.

## Small but perfectly formed

Archaeologists have done much to help determine just how equines have developed over millennia. Excavations in the ancient city of Pompeii, for example, have discovered many remains of donkeys and mules and, in 2018, the complete body of a horse lying where it was trapped in its stable as the weight of the volcanic ash from Mount Vesuvius covered all of this famous city. Their research was able to establish it was definitely the body of a horse rather than a donkey or mule but that, compared to the modern-day horse, it was quite small, standing at around 1.5 metres (4.9 feet) at the shoulder. Laura Geggel, writing for the popular science website Live Science, reported that, according to archaeologists with Parco Archeologico di Pompei, which excavated the site: '… it's likely that this horse was part of a noble breed of horses that took part in circus games and races during the time of the Roman Empire.'

Much closer to home, also in 2018, at Pocklington, East Yorkshire, archaeologists uncovered a Celtic site that included a grave dating sometime between 320 and 174 BC. The grave was found to contain not only the bones of a warrior but also personal artefacts, a chariot and the skeletons of two ponies. Although equines were rarely included in Iron Age burials, the fact that both ponies had been buried upright between the chariot shafts made the find even more unusual.

## Golden slippers

How and when horseshoes first began to be used around the world is open to conjecture. The ancient Greeks and some civilisations seemingly tried to protect the hooves of the animals which pulled their carts by either means of a boot laced around the hoof or with 'shoes' made from leather or rope. It's said that the Roman Emperor Nero had a chariot drawn by mules with shoes of silver while his consort Poppaea had her chariot team shod with shoes of gold.

Far more recently, before the advent of the motor lawnmower, a donkey was often used by many country house gardeners to pull a set of mowers. With an immaculate sward being the required result, the donkey's hooves were covered by specially made leather boots in order to prevent unwanted divots.

*A Little Bit of History*

## Who's in charge?

When living in a herd, it's often thought that it will be the strongest stallion that is in charge but some who have spent a great deal of time watching and understanding equines in a group situation consider that, a little like elephants in the wild, equines actually live in a matriarchal society. Ben Atkinson – of Atkinson Action Horses – gives amazing displays of horsemanship both nationally and internationally and is of the opinion that 'they will choose their lead mare because she makes the best decisions. When it rains, she takes them to shelter. When it's dry, she knows where the watering hole is. She's elected [by the herd] for her longstanding good decisions …'

## A mixing of breeds?

From *Country Life*, 18 September 1897:

> On Exmoor there are traditions about Spanish blood, and on Dartmoor they tell you of horses escaped from vessels belonging to the Spanish Armada which were wrecked on the coast of Devonshire. Nothing was more likely than that the ponies would stray over when they felt inclined for a change of run. But I think it by no means improbable that there has been a mixture of the breeds later than that, and of perhaps quite recent date. It is not a far cry from South Molton to Okehampton, the strip which divides the two moors, and what is more likely than that the two breeds should become mixed … Further south, however, they show more difference in type, and they are also on a bigger and sturdier scale … They are very hardy, and so they had need to be, as anyone who has ever been on Dartmoor on a bitter winter day with a northeast wind sweeping across it at top pace will scarcely require telling … No stallion over three years old is allowed on the moor, this perhaps being a survival of the old law of Henry VIII …

## Blood transfusion

In Britain there are several breeds of native ponies, among them the Dartmoor, Exmoor, Shetland, Eriskay, Welsh, Highland, Connemara, Fell, Dales and the New Forest. Although often referred to as being 'wild', they are in almost all instances, owned – and turned out to graze for much of the year on the moors and forests by people such as the 'commoners' of the New Forest. Periodic 'round-ups' or gatherings are held, during which the ponies are checked over; ownership established; the more mature foals separated from their mothers, and surplus animals are sold at auction, either as meat or to be broken as riding ponies.

To keep such native breeds genetically healthy, it was occasionally thought necessary by some owners of past generations to outcross their stock in order to introduce new, unrelated blood. As an example of this, in his book *Portrait of the New Forest* (Robert Hale & Co., 1966), author Brian Vesey-Fitzgerald notes:

> In 1891 the Association for the Improvement of the Breed of New Forest Ponies was founded with the object of awarding annual prizes and premiums to stallions after they had been passed by the Verderers to run in the Forest. In 1893 Lord Arthur Cecil, believing that the best way of ensuring improvement was by introducing fresh blood of other mountain and moorland breeds, began importing stallions from Dartmoor, Exmoor, the Fells, the Highlands and Wales ... for many years afterward, it can be safely said that the New Forest pony was a real mongrel. Moreover, the introduction of new blood was not always successful and there were many poor, weedy specimens in the Forest.

## Not so common

In the New Forest, a 'commoner' is someone who has land or property with ancient forest rights to 'depasture' or graze animals (cattle, ponies, donkeys, pigs and, in some areas, sheep) on the Forest. The rights stay with the property, not the person and not all houses come with rights so it's not as simple as buying a pony and just letting it out of the gate to do as it will. Helen Safe has lived in the New Forest all her life – and has commoners' rights: '… you have to brand it, be capable of going out and catching it if there is a problem (it took us eighteen months to catch one once!) and have somewhere suitable to keep it if it has to come in. A lot of houses with forest rights have no ground to go with them nowadays.'

Although Helen has traditional commoners' rights, she no longer allows her donkeys to graze where the public have access: 'There are real problems with the public feeding and encouraging them onto the roads – people used to queue up to buy ours ice creams from the shops and kiosks!'

## Drifting, learing and hefting

Anyone with ancient commoners' rights to graze livestock, in particular the native ponies of the New Forest, has a duty of care and, like all animal owners, a responsibility to ensure that their ponies are in good health at all times. In order to help ensure that they are, the verderers (based in Lyndhurst) employ agisters – whose duties include the well-being of all stock out on the Forest. In addition to this, they help arrange and organise the annual rounding up of ponies. The main purpose of these round-ups (known as 'drifts') is to drive the ponies and the current year's foals into stockade-type fenced areas where they can be checked over by their owners and the agister responsible for that particular area; wormed, weaned, marked with a brand specific to each commoner and be given a cut in the tail hair so that, when the ponies are rounded up again, the agisters know exactly where and when they were previously rounded up. Individuals may be taken from the herd to be sold or simply turned back out onto the Forest once all requirements have been satisfied.

To prevent individual herds of ponies roaming across the whole of Dartmoor, they are, over a period of generations (often as a result of foals learning from their mothers) conditioned to stay and graze within a fairly limited area. On Dartmoor this area is known as a 'lear' and animals staying on there are said to be 'learing' (not 'leering', which is another thing entirely!). In other parts of the UK, the practice is known as 'hefting' but the principles of this traditional way of keeping livestock in a certain area on open moorland or common land remain the same. Wherever it is carried out, successful learing or hefting means that it's possible for farmers or commoners to more easily locate and manage their stock.

## You can take a horse to water ...

Drifts and round-ups are not exclusive to the British countryside and there are many similar happenings concerning horses in all parts of the world. Possibly the biggest such occasion is the annual Chincoteague Pony Round-up, Swim and Auction which takes place on the last Wednesday and Thursday of July – and which, in 2025, celebrated its centenary. With thousands attending, it's certainly the largest as far as the numbers of spectators are concerned.

Similar to the Camargue in France, which is known for the wild horses that graze on the salt marshes, the Atlantic coastline of the Delmarva Peninsula between Maryland and Virginia is home to wild ponies which are rounded up from their grazing grounds on Assateague Island and swum across the water to neighbouring Chincoteague Island. There is tradition as well as practicality attached to the occasion and a part of that tradition is that the first foal ashore is named King or Queen Neptune and given away in a fundraising raffle. The monies raised from this and other events held over the two days of the round-up helps fund the care and well-being of the pony herds, with a portion also going to the local volunteer fire service.

## Wild and worldwide

Elsewhere in America, native wild horses primarily graze in ten western states (Arizona, California, Colorado, Idaho, Montana, Nevada, New Mexico, Oregon, Utah and Wyoming) on government-designated Herd Management Areas (HMAs). There are also feral herds of donkeys (often referred to locally as 'burros') not native to North America but which are thought to have originated from imported animals descended from the African wild ass. In certain areas their increasing numbers are becoming a problem and, in places like Death Valley, cause damage to vegetation, spring ecosystems and compete with native wildlife.

Australia is said to be home to the world's largest population of feral/wild horses (estimates say 'up to 400,000') and, as in the case cited above, they are causing ecological damage in some of the more sensitive areas of the Australian Alps – including the Alpine and Kosciuszko National Parks. In the Netherlands – at the rewilding/nature reserves of the Oostvaardersplassen, Konick horses (which originally roamed wild in Poland and Belarus) were brought in to aid with habitat management but were so successful in their breeding that they became overstocked and their grazing grounds proved insufficient to sustain them. It was an intolerable situation and so many were transported back to reserves in Belarus and to Spain.

Breeds of ponies being imported from other countries in order to facilitate various rewilding projects in Britain are frowned upon by some – their argument being that the native breeds are more suitable for the terrain and topography the rewilders are hoping to establish. There is also concern that, in places designated Sites of Special Scientific Interest (SSSIs), numbers of wild or feral ponies (which some maintain are not wild at all but abandoned without any method of owner identification such as passport, microchip or tattoo) are becoming too numerous and therefore detrimental to the habitat.

# 3

# FICTION AND SUPERSTITION

Over the doors of many stables, tack rooms and outbuildings hangs an old horseshoe positioned there for good luck. The superstition is said to have arisen as a result of the legend of how, when the Devil asked St Dunstan to shoe his cloven hooves, the not-so-saintly saint purposefully hurt him. In exchange for mercy, the Devil promised never again to enter any place where a horseshoe is displayed. Some might add that the iron contained within the shoe will ward off all evil spirits.

In the UK any horseshoe intended for such a purpose should always be hung with the gap to the top otherwise – so it is commonly believed – all the good luck will run out of it. Not so in France and, should you ever be charged with fixing a horseshoe in a similar position across the Channel, it must be placed upside down. Likewise in some parts of America. In Wyoming, for instance, it's said that, when positioned over the workplace of a farrier, the good luck gained from an inverted horseshoe runs directly onto the blacksmith's anvil.

## Favourite hobby horse

The definition of 'hobby horse' (according to the *Pocket Oxford Dictionary*) is either a 'child's toy consisting of a stick with a horse's head' or a person's 'favourite subject or idea'. In the late sixteenth and early seventeenth centuries however, the definition could also include a small Irish breed of horse; the wickerwork-and-costume dancing equine effigy so often used as a morris dancing accessory, and also refer to 'wanton women and fools'.

## Is this you?
Power, beauty and freedom symbolise the horse in the Chinese culture. People born in the year of the horse are meant to be very high-spirited, active and energetic. Their enthusiasm and cheerful personalities make people like them. Those born in the year of the horse are said to like to be the centre of attention and make everyone around them enjoy their company!

## Superstitious donkey data

- The Bible says that a donkey was the mode of transport used by Jesus for his journey into Jerusalem on Palm Sunday – and, according to legend, is the reason why many have darker hair in the shape of a cross on their back.
- According to some Devon folklore of old, the best way to cure a child of whooping cough was to bring a donkey to the door of your home and thrust a slice of bread in its mouth. (History fails to reveal whether a certain type of bread was required or if a loaf of Mother's Pride would do!) Then, according to those in the know, the sick infant had simply to be passed three times over and under the animal's body in order to effect an almost immediate recovery.

## Things that go bump in the knight
Berry Pomeroy Castle near Paignton, Devon, is purported to be one of England's most-haunted places, with sightings of long-gone ladies, spectral soldiers and maligned maidens being regularly

observed over the centuries. Legend meets fact on occasion but, in one particular instance, although the story has its origins in a real-life event, there appears to be no historical evidence pertaining to the demise of two brothers and their horses.

In 1549 Edward VI held the Pomeroy family responsible for a religious rebellion and, as a result, ordered his troops to seize the castle. However, to save themselves from the ignominy of defeat, it's said that two sons of the family dressed in their knights' armour, blindfolded their horses before mounting and then rode them to the top of the ramparts where they spurred the poor animals over the edge and into the deep valley below. Unsurprisingly, all were killed on impact and the area over which they rode became known as Pomeroy's Leap – from where, so it is said, screams and the sound of heavy impact comparable to the thuds of horses and riders hitting the ground can sometimes be heard.

## Bloody goings-on

One way or another horses (and ponies and donkeys) have suffered immeasurably at the hands of their owners and handlers – both now and in the past. At one time, on St Stephen's Day (26 December/Boxing Day) it was common practice for horsemen to 'bleed' their animals thinking that doing so would help in keeping horses strong and healthy during the coming year. The practice was an ancient one derived from the belief that drawing off 'old' blood (often as much as two or three pints via a knife incision in the animal's gum) was beneficial. In contemporary reports of the times, not much was said about the dangers of infection or even anaemia resulting from such goings-on but, given the less than sanitary conditions of the average standard of stabling of the time, such side effects must surely have been fairly commonplace.

## A comeuppance for cruelty
Spectral and supposedly mystical horses appear in many legends and superstitions in all parts of the British Isles, particularly on moorland or in wide, wild, open spaces. Dartmoor has several which supposedly appear (quite often mounted by a ghostly rider) in front of weary travellers and, in Scottish folklore, the Grey Mare of Ballachulish is said to appear on misty nights. As to who might be unfortunate enough to witness her appearance, one explanation has it that she is only ever seen by humans who have been cruel to their animals and that she is seeking revenge after herself being horribly mistreated by a cruel and spiteful owner.

## Don't take their word for it
In the past, on or around 11 November (Martinmas), a type of initiation ceremony for young men taking on the role of ploughman or other horsemen's duties on the land took place annually in various parts of the British Isles. Once completed – and after having been sworn to secrecy, the initiates were said to have joined the Society of Horsemen and were given the 'Word', which supposedly gave them positive powers over the horses in their charge. As to the animals themselves, some of the concoctions given as a result of advice offered during impartation of the Word would have done them no good at all. There are, for instance, accounts of ingredients such as soap, turpentine, tobacco, sulphur, hellebore and even small particles of iron filings being made into pills and potions intended to 'condition' and/or 'purify' the horse. In several instances (unsurprisingly, given the nature of some of the ingredients), it is known that the opposite effect was achieved.

On occasion, a magic potion was supposed to be sufficient to stop horses from breaking out of a field. In his 1979 book, *Horse Power and Magic*, author and countryman George Ewart Evans mentions that a certain Walter Cater from Redgrave in Suffolk had benefited from some of the secrets handed down in the Horseman's Word and, as a result, was able to keep his horses in a meadow for up to five days by the simple expedient of slathering a strong-smelling concoction on nearby trees and boundary posts.

More generally in East Anglia, it was thought that a secret ritual involving a particular bone from a toad would give the men who performed it the ability to handle horses (it was also said to give them power over women but that's a subject for another book!). Obtaining the required bone from a toad was complicated. Having caught and killed your toad, it needed to be dried out overnight (preferably on a blackthorn tree) before then being buried for a month in an anthill – after which time, the skeleton was picked out and washed in a moonlit stream until the crotch bone 'rose and floated uphill against the current'. This all-important bone is/was, significantly enough, shaped like a horse's hoof and had then to be baked and ground into a powder – which was mixed with other ingredients to make a 'jading oil' said to 'bewitch horses'.

## Benign beliefs?

Sometimes owners of horses and ponies which mainly live out and graze the fields at night-time, are alarmed by the sight of an unexplained plait in their animal's mane and tail, the appearance of which has nothing to do with them. The most common fear is that it has been put there as a marker with a view to the horse being stolen in the near future but, according to the experiences of many rural police forces that is unlikely to be the case. Instead, their favoured theory is that some of the gods worshipped by warlocks and white witches have strong connections to equines and that placing plaits in a horse's mane or tail increases the strength between them. It is supposedly a benign activity but to discover one left in the mane of their horse or pony is understandably worrying for their owner. When these plaits might suddenly appear often depends on the time of year and its proximity to certain dates important to white witchcraft and worship – such as, according to Sussex Horsewatch (www.sussexhorsewatch.webs.com):

> Imbolc (2 February); spring equinox (20 March); Beltane (30 May); summer solstice (21 June) [and] Lughnasadh (31 July) … Samhain (31 October) and winter solstice (21 December). There may also be other dates when the plaiting happens that are personal to a particular 'witch'. Full moons may also be used if she is performing a particular piece of magic.

One might wonder why those concerned don't just ask the horse owner's permission but apparently to do so would weaken the spell if they were to speak of it to others not in the 'circle'.

## It's all in the cards

Horses have long held significant meaning in various cultures throughout history. In the realm of tarot readings, equines of one description or another appear in the cards no less than seven times – some signify better luck than others but, in general, their appearance seems to suggest that life will take a forward step and positive progress, encouraging action and change. Depending on how the horse features on any particular card, it may, however, be warning you to take care and not rush blindly into certain situations as you move forward. Like dressage and many other horse-related disciplines, it's all a question of balance and control.

# 4

# FAMOUS HORSES

Over the years – nay centuries – there have been many horses and ponies who have made a name for themselves in a variety of ways. Songster was one of the most decorated horses in the First World War who, after being brought back to Britain, drew a milk float, hunted with the Quorn hounds, regularly accompanied his owner Bert Main to the local pub and, on dying aged forty (in 1940), was buried with the medals (Mons Star, 1914–1915 Star, General Service Medal, Victory Medal, plus two long-service medals) earned during conflict.

**Not tonight, Marengo!**
Désirée, a light grey Arabian mare, is far less well known as being Napoleon's horse than is Marengo who, although not much more than a pony was, by contemporary accounts, 'a reliable and courageous mount'. Wounded eight times in battle, Marengo was also used as a courier from Valladolid to Burgos – a distance of 80 miles – and in a time of five hours there and back. Captured at the Battle of Waterloo and transported back to the UK, he died at the age of thirty-eight and his skeleton is on display in the National Army Museum (minus one hoof which was turned into a snuff box!).

As something of an aside, although Napoleon was depicted as being astride a magnificent charger in the painting *Napoleon Crossing the Alps* – one of five oil on canvas portraits of the emperor undertaken between 1801 and 1805 by French artist, Jacques-Louis David – it's thought in some quarters that Napoleon's actual four-legged companion on that particular occasion was almost certainly a mule and that the portrait was a result of pure artistic licence created for the purpose of propaganda.

There is also an interesting footnote regarding Marengo's name. According to historian Dr Jean-François Lemaire: 'The French archives are silent about Marengo' and it has been suggested that it was a nickname given to another horse by Napoleon – who was, by all accounts, quite prone to giving alternative names to both humans and horses of whom he was fond.

Another of Napoleon's mounts – and one whose name has been verified – was Le Vizir, an Arabian stallion gifted to the emperor by an Ottoman sultan in 1802. Branded on his rump with the initial 'N' topped with a crown, Le Vizir was apparently cared for in the Imperial stables after Napoleon's 1814 abdication until the horse's death, aged thirty-three, in 1826. Treated to the skills of a taxidermist and stuffed, Le Vizir appears to have had equally as interesting and unusual journey in death as he did in life, being variously kept in northern France and, at one stage, being transported to England and put on show by the Manchester Natural History Society. Having eventually been repatriated to France, poor old Le Vizir was restuffed and, in 2017 a successful crowd-funding appeal enabled him to be fully restored at the Army Museum in Paris.

## Wonderful, wonderful Copenhagen

Like Napoleon's Marengo, the Duke of Wellington's horse Copenhagen was not much more than a pony in height and became the mount of the 'Iron Duke' by default when it was realised that the animal would never, as his breeder had initially hoped, become a viable racehorse.

Wellington and his mount soon became an easily recognised sight on the battlefield; perhaps most famously when, as mentioned on the horse's tombstone to be found at Stratfield Saye, Hampshire, Copenhagen was: 'The charger ridden by the Duke of Wellington the entire day at the Battle of Waterloo.' Of their partnership, Wellington said: 'I rode him throughout the rest of the war ... There may have been many faster horses, no doubt many handsomer, but for bottom and endurance I never saw the like of the fellow.' The duke may, however, have been looking back through rose-tinted spectacles as it's said that, after Waterloo and seventeen hours on the battlefield, when Wellington went to pat him, 'the exhausted stallion lashed out' at his rider.

Copenhagen's fame continued long after he had returned home from battle – in 1828, when Wellington was elected prime minister, he chose to ride Copenhagen to the door of 10 Downing Street and when the horse died some eight years later, he was accorded military honours at his burial in the grounds of the duke's home in Hampshire.

## An extraordinary horse with a very ordinary name

> Half a league, half a league,
> Half a league onward,
> All in the valley of Death
> Rode the six hundred.
> 'Forward, the Light Brigade!
> Charge for the guns!' he said.
> Into the valley of Death
> Rode the six hundred.

On 25 October 1854, the Light Brigade, led by Lord Cardigan, mounted a frontal (and, as it turned out, extremely disastrous) assault against a Russian artillery battery. Although Cardigan is often mentioned, the charger he was riding at the time is less credited in accounts.

Given the unremarkable name of Ronald, the horse which led the charge (made famous by the poem of Alfred, Lord Tennyson) was a 15.2hh thoroughbred chestnut gelding. It was little comfort in the scheme of things but happily, Ronald survived the 'valley of Death' – unlike 475 other horses out of the original 673 that went into battle.

Foaled and reared at the 7th Earl of Cardigan's Deene Park estate, near Corby, Northamptonshire, on returning home after Balaclava, Ronald lived four years longer than his rider and died in June 1872. Visitors to Deene Park today can see a portrait of Lord Cardigan and Ronald hanging over the dining room fireplace.

## Warrior – the real 'War Horse'

While there have already been several references made to the book and film, *War Horse* (and there are more to come!), it is perhaps worth reminding readers that Joey the horse and his survival of the First World War is based on Warrior, the mount of General Jack Seely, the Lord Mottistone.

Brought more to public knowledge in the twenty-first century because of Morpurgo's book, the stage play and film, Warrior was already a legend in his lifetime and his death even warranted obituaries in the mainstream press – just one of which was this, from 4 April 1941 edition of the *Evening Standard*:

> Lord Mottistone's famous old war horse Warrior, which he ... rode during the last war, has died at Mottistone Manor, Isle of Wight, at the age of thirty-two.

Warrior had so many narrow escapes from death in the last war that the Canadian cavalry, whom Lord Mottistone commanded in France, used to call him 'the horse the Germans can't kill'.

## The Lloyds Bank black horse

While few know their names, many know the various black horses that have, since 1989, featured in the famous Lloyds Bank television advertisements. The very first of these was Cancara, a Trakehner stallion who was bred by Marian Hewitt and subsequently owned by Graham Parker, a television cameraman and producer. Cancara represented the bank in further adverts – including one where he is seen apparently rearing by the side of a waterfall. However, things are not always as they seem and, such is the wizardry of technology, the horse was first filmed rearing then the image was superimposed onto a waterfall backdrop constructed at Pinewood Studios in Iver Heath, Buckinghamshire. Becoming something of a celebrity, Cancara made publicity appearances at charity events, shop openings and several agricultural shows before his death in June 2006, aged thirty-one.

Other horses featuring in Lloyds Bank adverts have included Dante, Tarantino, Imperator and Prokofiev and, in the seventh (which first aired in the spring of 2023), six very similar-looking horses were used for most of the sequences – with a total of twelve appearing in the final scene.

### *A financial incentive*

The first recorded use of the black horse sign was in 1677, but it was not until 1884 that it began to be used by Lloyds Bank. As both their logo and an advertising medium, it has worked incredibly well and there are some banking with Lloyds today who only began doing so as a result of being persuaded by the incentive of a black horse money box which was, several years ago, offered as promotional gift to children opening a savings account with Lloyds.

## Red Rum

Although also mentioned in the 'Equine Epitaphs' chapter, it is well worth recording the name of Red Rum here. After winning the Grand National three times, and coming second in the race twice, the horse became something of a national treasure during the 1970s.

In October 2022, marking the 27th anniversary of his death, *Horse & Hound* published an article written by Julian Muscat who commented on the less than auspicious beginnings of Red Rum's career – and the subsequent rags-to-riches story:

> Red Rum was an anonymous seven-year-old when he was bought by a small-time trainer from Lancashire in 1972. Originally a second-hand car dealer, Ginger McCain gave 6,000gns for a fifth-hand horse he housed in rundown stables behind his used-car showroom in the sleepy suburb of Birkdale.
>
> Red Rum was a virtual cripple from the day he arrived, yet Ginger saw hope where others had despaired. In his taxi-driving days, he'd befriended a regular customer in Noel le Mare, whose dream it was to win the Grand National.
>
> Time was fast running out for Noel, who was eighty-four at the time. So Ginger badgered him until he relented. Noel would give Ginger funds to buy a horse which saw Red Rum join the other equine renegades under Ginger's wing ...

Red Rum was pensioned off from racing in 1978 – and so great were his achievements that reports of his retirement made the front page of many newspapers. However, in subsequent years, he returned to Aintree in order to lead the parade of horses before the Grand National and, as can be seen from television and YouTube footage, absolutely loved the attention. Like Cancara, the horse which featured in the Lloyds Bank television adverts (see previous mention), Red Rum also became something of an equine celebrity, often being called upon to open supermarkets and attend other public events.

## 'A clue ... that is what we haven't got.'

Over the years since his disappearance so much has been written in newspaper articles, books and online regarding Shergar and his abduction from the stables at the Ballymany Stud in February 1983 that to write more here is possibly superfluous. He can, however, be most definitely considered a 'famous horse' so it would be wrong to omit him in this compilation of names.

Bred in Country Kildare, Ireland, by the Aga Khan, Shergar won his debut race as a three-year-old at Sandown by ten lengths. He won the Chester Vase (run at Chester Racecourse) by twelve and, in the same year, the Epsom Derby by another ten. The Irish Derby saw Shergar first past the winning post and so, cashing in on his success, the Aga Khan sold shares in the horse – thirty-four of them, each for £250,000. He retained six shares for himself (making the horse potentially worth £10 million) and put the stallion to stud. Although thirty-five mares put to Shergar in his first season produced foals, the opportunity to prove himself further never materialised as before he could, he was kidnapped by a group of – according to groom James Fitzgerald – 'at least six armed men wearing balaclavas'. One of the most popular theories is that they were members of the Provisional Irish Republican Army who were after a ransom to be paid by the Aga Khan.

Given the huge public interest (somewhat akin to that of the mysterious disappearance of Lord Lucan in 1974), police investigation was done under the close scrutiny of the media – and the failure to find the horse, or indeed, any leads as to his whereabouts, gave rise to the kidnapping being referred to as a 'caricature of police bungling' with Chief Superintendent Jim Murphy famously telling reporters when asked if there were any clues regarding the abduction: 'A clue … that is what we haven't got.'

## Perhaps not-so Clever Hans?

Ask some in the research and scientific world to explain 'the observer-expectancy effect' and they might well respond by saying: 'The observer-expectancy effect occurs when researchers influence the results of their own study through interactions with participants. Researchers' own beliefs and expectations about the study results may unintentionally influence participants through demand characteristics' – all of which apparent gobbledygook is likely to cause some readers here to wonder 'what on earth might this have to do with horses?' Well, such thinking spawned an offshoot known by some as the 'Clever Hans effect' – which is linked entirely to the fact that Hans, an Orlov trotter stallion, was, for several years during the latter part of the nineteenth century and into the very early years of the twentieth, apparently able to answer mathematical and other intellectual tasks posed by his handler, Wilhelm von Osten. An entry in www.britannica.com explains more:

> In exhibitions beginning in 1891 … Hans would demonstrate almost 'human' intelligence by responding to questions with a variety of hoof taps or other actions. Using this method, Hans amazed both the general public and leading psychologists of the day with his apparent ability to perform arithmetic functions, identify colours, read and spell, and even identify musical tones. A number of investigators examined the horse and handler and

concluded that no voluntary signals were being given to the horse, and that led many to suppose that Hans's apparent mental abilities were real.

Not all were convinced and a formal investigation conducted in 1907 as to the veracity of Clever Hans's intelligence concluded that the horse was actually responding directly to involuntary cues from the body language of von Osten. Since that time (again referencing www.britannica.com): 'behavioural researchers have referred to the "Clever Hans effect" to denote the danger of unintentional cueing of the desired behaviour by the questioner if experiments are not carefully designed.'

## Across Spain with a donkey

In 1879, Robert Louis Stevenson, author of many fictional books (*Treasure Island*; *Kidnapped*; *The Strange Case of Dr Jekyll and Mr Hyde*), wrote a true account of a journey which he and a donkey named Modestine took through Spain. Apparently bought for the sum of sixty-five francs and a glass of brandy, in *Travels with a Donkey in the Cévennes* (published in 1879), Stevenson talks of Modestine being 'not much bigger than a dog' and 'the colour of a mouse'. Despite any human/equine affinity which may have evolved during the journey, the writer nevertheless sold Modestine at St Jean de Gaard after twelve days and travelling 120 miles.

Over 125 years later, Robert Louis Stevenson's trek across Spain in the company of a donkey inspired journalist and author Tim Moore to attempt something similar. Moore's plan was to walk the pilgrims' route to Santiago de Compostela so, with much trepidation and having looked at several donkeys which, for one reason or another, failed their auditions, he eventually bought an animal named Shinto for the sum of 800 euros. Whether or not, as was the case with Stevenson and Modestine, a glass of brandy was included in the transaction, the author fails to relate. The couple's exploits are, however, very amusingly covered in Moore's 2004 book, *Spanish Steps: Travels With My Donkey*, which, as the jacket blurb states: '... is the story of what happens when a rather silly man tries to walk all the way across a very large country, with a very large animal who doesn't really want to.' And, for those who might be wondering what happened to Shinto at the end of the adventure, well, Tim gifted him back to his original owner.

## Black Bess

Most people know the story of the legendary highwayman Dick Turpin and his horse Black Bess but, in actual fact, Black Bess never existed and, rather than being a romantic figure of history, Turpin was a cruel and merciless robber and murderer.

An article featured as part of the British Library's website in 'Discovering Literature: Romantics and Victorians collection items' tells the reader that *Black Bess, or, The Knight of the road: a tale of the good old times* was published between 1866 and 1868 as 'a heavily fictionalised account of the life and death of the infamous English highway bandit' – and includes the story of Turpin riding Black Bess the 200 miles between York and London in a single night.

Turpin's legendary marathon ride (from Kent – not London – to York) was inspired by a real-life ride undertaken by John 'Swift Nick' Nevison some decades earlier and was an attempt to provide himself with an alibi. Arriving at York, Nevison stabled his obviously exhausted horse at an inn and, having changed to clean clothes, laid a bet at a bowls match and had conversations with several townspeople. As the distance he had travelled in the time seemed so impossible, his presence in York was sufficient for him not to be thought guilty of a robbery in Kent.

As a follow-up to this, although it wasn't Turpin who rode the distance, he did, nevertheless, go north (he was eventually captured and hanged in York) and, to make money, began stealing horses and selling them on under the alias of 'John Palmer'.

*There it was – gone!*
Incidental, yet tenuously relevant to the subject of horse stealers of Dick Turpin's ilk, some might be amused by an exchange of conversation included in an episode of BBC Television's *Peaky Blinders* series – a popular British period drama following the exploits of a Birmingham-based crime gang operating immediately after the First World War:

'What was your father's profession?'

'Well, he told fortunes and stole horses … Often he would tell a man that his horse would be stolen, and they would marvel at his powers when it was.'

## Famous by association

Few will remember a chestnut horse named Black Jack – until that is, they are reminded of American president John F. Kennedy's funeral and the emotional sight of the riderless horse being led along behind the cortège as it processed from the Capitol to St Matthew's Church and then to Arlington Cemetery. Although without a rider, Black Jack was kitted out with saddle and bridle – and attached to the saddle was a sheathed sword plus, in the stirrups, reversed boots, symbolism indicating that 'a leader had fallen and would ride no more'.

Equally emotional was the moment when in Britain, on 19 September 2022, as the late Queen Elizabeth's coffin was being carried in a hearse up the flower-strewn Long Walk at Windsor Castle, Emma, one of Her Majesty's favourite Fell ponies was seen standing quietly alongside head groom, Terry Pendry. The pony seemed to have her head bowed as the procession passed by and that, combined with the fact that the late Queen's headscarf (which she had several times been seen wearing as she was photographed riding in the grounds of Windsor) was laid folded over the saddle was enough to induce tears in the eyes of even the most hard-hearted of onlookers.

## Burmese – steady under fire

Although those of a younger generation will only ever have seen her in a horse-drawn carriage, some of a certain age might well remember when Queen Elizabeth II rode (side-saddle) on her horse Burmese in order to lead the parade and take the salute at the annual ceremony of Trooping the Colour – an event that traditionally celebrates the reigning monarch's official birthday.

Burmese, a black thoroughbred mare foaled at Fort Walsh, Saskatchewan, was gifted to Queen Elizabeth by the Royal Canadian Mounted Police and was ridden by her in eighteen consecutive Trooping the Colours between 1969 and 1986. In 1981, an incident as the Queen was heading towards Horse Guards Parade from Buckingham Palace and up The Mall proved both the careful training of Burmese by the Canadian Mounted Police and also Her Majesty's proficiency as a horsewoman. A BBC report from 13 June 1981, under the headline: 'Queen shot at by youth', told readers that

> A 17-year-old man has been arrested for shooting a replica gun at the Queen as she rode past crowds on horseback. Marcus Serjeant pointed a pistol directly at the Queen as she turned down Horse Guards Parade for the start of the Trooping the Colour ceremony. He fired six blank cartridges before being overcome by a guardsman and police. The shots ... startled the Queen's horse, but she was able to bring it back under control within a few seconds.

Neither horse nor rider were injured and Serjeant was subsequently found guilty of 'wilfully discharging at the person of Her Majesty the Queen a blank cartridge pistol, with intent to alarm her' and under the 1842 Treason Act, jailed for five years – but was released in October 1984. As for Burmese, she was eventually retired to Windsor Castle where she died in 1990 aged twenty-eight.

## Juno – banging the drum for equality

At Trooping the Colour and at many other state and public ceremonial occasions, the Household Cavalry Mounted Regiment (a union of the Life Guards and the Blues and Royals, the two most senior regiments in the British Army) are generally accompanied by the band of the Household Cavalry – at the very front of which can usually be seen the huge horses (most often piebald, skewbald or roan in colour) bearing silver kettle drums. Traditionally, the larger drum of the two each horse carries was placed on the right – a consideration which allows the drummer's stronger right hand to play the main beat. However, as both the rider's hands are busily occupied in 'banging the drum', the horses are controlled with reins operated via the stirrups.

Having drum horses leading the band is said to date back to 1660. Each of the horses thus used throughout generations have been given the rank of 'Major'; in addition to which, they tend to be given monikers taken from classical mythology. In 2023, Juno was the first drum horse to be officially named in the reign of King Charles III and Queen Camilla – and has also found fame in being the first ever mare to have been enlisted as a drum horse. Previously named Willa Rose, she was presented to Queen Camilla at a small ceremony in the gardens of Clarence House in June 2023 after two years of training in readiness for a potential long life of public pomp and circumstance.

## Sefton – famous for all the wrong reasons

In July 1982, a troop of horses and riders heading towards Changing the Guard duties at Whitehall were blasted by a car bomb planted by the IRA and detonated via remote control. Seven of the sixteen horses were killed with seven more being seriously injured. Among the seven, was Sefton whose injuries from the blast were colossal: he had several wounds to his neck from metal car parts, a severed jugular vein from a further piece of debris, damage to his stifle and flanks, five 4-inch nails embedded in his face and a damaged cornea in his burnt right eye. In total, thirty-eight wounds of differing severity. If the shock and loss of blood didn't cause his demise then – or so the Army veterinary surgeons thought at the time – the extent of his injuries most certainly would. Thankfully, their skill and Sefton's tenacity ensured that he eventually recovered.

The bombing horrified most of the British public who saw the aftermath of the explosion on both television and the front pages of their newspapers – and Sefton soon became something of a hero, especially when, after his wounds had healed, he returned to duty before finally being retired in October 1984. It was a retirement he seemingly enjoyed, living another nine years until, in July 1993, aged thirty, he was put to sleep because of lameness thought to have been a result of his injuries. He was buried at the Defence Animal Centre, Melton Mowbray, where a marble headstone marks the spot.

# 5

# EQUINE EPITAPHS

In addition to relatively modern memorials to horses such as Sefton (as described at the end of the previous chapter), if one cares to look around the churchyards and churches of Britain, particularly those in England, there appears to be a strong connection between man and horse. A headstone at Blyford, Suffolk, dated 1849 commemorates the life (and death) of twenty-one-year-old ploughman Samuel Croft and contains a relief of two horses being unharnessed from the plough, a symbol of his labours in the field being over.

Elsewhere it is quite possible to see an image of a horse alongside an effigy of its owner. Sometimes these are incidental to the person being commemorated but at other times, such as the monument to Colonel Edward Hawkins Cheney in St Luke's Church, Gaddesby, Lincolnshire, it's the horse that has the greater significance. Colonel Cheney (of the Scots Greys) is depicted with Tanner – one of the five horses that were shot from under him at the Battle of Waterloo.

Other memorials to horses are far less ostentatious; sometimes they are little more than a stone onto which have been chiselled a few words. One such can be found by the eagle-eyed walking the mile-long tree-lined avenue (apparently created in 1641 by Sir Thomas Tomkins to celebrate becoming a member of parliament) at Monnington Court in the Wye Valley. Tucked into the grass – often overgrown depending on the time of year – is a small headstone dedicated to:

Springervale
Pecora
1971–1996
Great Show Horse and Lifter of the Spirit

A small, seemingly inconsequential headstone it may be but, as with many things, there is a far bigger story hidden behind the chiselled script.

Pecora was a mare of the Morgan breed owned by famous sculptor and artist Angela Conner Bulmer – and lived at Monnington Court. In 1975, she brought three Morgan horses from America; the three being, according to a *New York Times* article in February of that year, 'the first of their breed to be imported by Britain'. Given the dates of both the newspaper account and those on the headstone, it is quite likely that Pecora was one of the three. Whether she was or not, Angela Conner Bulmer is to be credited for having started the Morgan horse registry in the UK. The *New York Times* article quoted her as saying:

> I've been fascinated by Morgans ever since I first saw one [in America] back in 1965 … I've been looking around the United States for four years and must have checked out thousands of Morgans before I found just what I wanted … The reason I looked for so long was that every Morgan produced in Britain in the future will have the bloodline to these horses, so, of course, I wanted them to be the best.

As an aside, the American bloodlines suffered a loss as a result of a tragic accident befalling the Morgan mares belonging to a Mr Phillips of Windsor, Vermont. Well known as an influential breeder, in the late 1800s several of his herd were killed by a freak lightning strike as they were grazing in a pasture. Two stallions and 'a few mares' were, however, in a horse barn elsewhere and survived as a consequence. It was these animals that would become the nucleus of a breeding programme organised by a Robert Lippitt Knight after the death of their previous owner – and who used the stud prefix 'Lippitt' on all the stock he subsequently bred.

## Head towards the winning post

Red Rum is the only horse to have won three Grand Nationals (1973, 1974 and 1977) – and to have come second twice in that particular race. Already mentioned in 'Famous Horses' (see the previous chapter), so well loved was he by both the general public and serious racegoers that, after dying in October 1995 at the age of thirty, this hero of the racetrack was given the unique honour of being buried near the finishing line at Aintree with, appropriately enough, his head facing the winning post. A small headstone nearby records his three wins and two second places in the National.

## Over the Rainbow Bridge

In recent years it has become commonplace to read – particularly on social media – when announcing the death of a beloved animal, be it horse, dog, cat or whatever a person's chosen pet, that he or she has 'gone over the Rainbow Bridge'. The origin of the saying is unclear but perhaps it comes from the idea of the Bifröst bridge of Norse mythology – believed to have been a burning bridge reaching between 'Midgard' (Earth) and 'Asgard' (heaven and the realm of the gods). The expression may, though, have been brought into modern usage as a result of a poem called 'The Rainbow Bridge'. Who wrote it is debatable: some credit Paul Dahm, a grief councillor from Oregon, America; others seem to favour a certain Scottish teenager named Edna Clyne. Whatever the truth, the expression has come to be a sort of sentimental verbal or written memorial to horses and other animals loved and lost.

## Beware Chalk Pit – a monument to a horse

At Farley Mount, near Winchester, Hampshire, there is a rather splendid pyramid-shaped monument to a horse which, in the eighteenth century, had a name change because of a quite remarkable incident. As the inscription in an alcove within the monument explains:

> Underneath lies buried a horse, the property of Paulet St John Esq., that in the month of September 1733 leaped into a chalk pit twenty-five feet deep a foxhunting with his master on his back and in October 1734 he won the Hunters Plate on Worthy Downs and was rode by his owner and was entered in the name of 'Beware Chalk Pit'.

It's often suggested that the monument dates from 1795, but some historians claim that it must have been erected prior to 1772 as Paulet St John (a member of parliament and one-time mayor of Winchester) was awarded a baronetcy that year and the inscription on the plaque fails to mention that fact – which it would almost certainly do. There's also some doubt about the name-change as a scribe researching for the *Sporting Magazine* of 1840 was of the opinion that the horse was better known as Foxhunter – so perhaps was entered in the race at Winchester under the name of Beware Chalk Pit as a tongue-in-cheek gesture.

*Equine Epitaphs*

## Roadside remembrance

Staying in Hampshire, if you were to travel along the section of the A272 that runs eastwards from Winchester towards Petersfield, about 1½ miles out of Bramdean and 2½ miles before the West Meon Hut traffic lights, there's a turning to the right signposted Brockwood and Brockwood Park School. Take that turning and almost immediately look to the roadside on your left. Here stands the memorial (not much bigger than an old-fashioned milestone) to Melksham, a horse belonging to a certain Colonel Richard Meinertzhagen.

Local knowledge has it that when Melksham fatally fell at the roadside, Meinertzhagen (born in 1878 and a pupil at Harrow during the same period as Winston Churchill) had the horse buried exactly where he had died and commemorated his life with a simple headstone – on which is chiselled:

Here Lies Col. R Meinertzhagen's
Horse
Melksham
Buried under these stones
Who died at this place in
1910

## *The Melksham Hoard*

As a very tenuous link to the name of Meinertzhagen's deceased mount – but horse-related nonetheless – it is perhaps worth mentioning that, as part of the Melksham Hoard discovered in Wiltshire in 1972, there were three copper alloy horse harness fittings (known by archaeologists and historians as 'phalera') which dated to the early Iron Age. They were discovered among the spoil generated during the diversion of the river Avon for the Melksham bypass.

## Heart and soul

In her marvellous book *Palaces for Pigs* (English Heritage, 2011), writer, photographer and broadcaster Lucinda Lambton tells of a small memorial on the village green at Latimer, Buckinghamshire, which commemorates a French horse who served during the Boer War's Battle of Boshof. The horse had originally belonged to a French mercenary with the incredibly grand-sounding name of George Henri Anne-Marie Victor de Villebois-Mareuil. The length and grandeur of his name was not, however, apparently sufficient defence against Lord Chesham and his troops during the battle and, after fighting bravely, he was killed. His mount, however, had more luck. As Lucinda Lambton mentions: 'His horse, a small dark Arab, had been wounded and Lord Chesham determined that it should be nursed back to health; so it was, in Buckinghamshire. Renamed Villebois, it was to live at Latimer for another eleven years. When the horse died, its heart, along with its ceremonial trappings, was buried ... on the village green.'

## Foxhunter – gone to ground

Sir Harry Llewellyn and his horse Foxhunter (also mentioned briefly in Chapter 18, 'A Clear Round') won the King George V Gold Cup three times (1948, 1950 and 1953) and an Olympic gold medal at Helsinki in 1952. The victorious combination of animal and human has been ascribed to the fact that Foxhunter was 'an exceptional horse whose big heart, bravery and drive', ideally matched with a rider who had 'skill, flair and insight'.

Foxhunter died in 1959 and, as recorded in Wikipedia: 'His skeleton was preserved and donated to the Royal Veterinary College, where it was put on permanent display in the college's Anatomy Museum. Foxhunter's hide was buried on the Blorenge Mountain between Abergavenny and Blaenavon.' It's an area popular with walkers and all who want to enjoy the views from a Welsh hillside so, whether deliberate or pure coincidence, there is a car park in close proximity of Foxhunter's memorial – on which is a plaque listing his achievements. Harry Llewellyn (who had farmed and owned land nearby) died in 1999 and, appropriately enough, given his connection with both the horse and surrounding countryside, his ashes were scattered over the Blorenge.

## Size isn't everything

If one were ever to take a walk around the golf course at Barton-on-Sea, Hampshire, you might just notice the memorial to Marion Mould (née Coakes)'s horse Stroller, close to where he is buried overlooking the Solent and the Isle of Wight. The pair competed in the 1968 Olympics in Mexico and Stroller – given his size – more accurately a pony rather than a horse, is perhaps the only pony ever to have successfully participated at the Olympics in a showjumping event. The golf course used to be part of the farm which was owned by Marion's family, but the golf club has kept the headstone and honoured Stroller by naming a tee after him.

Fond memories of his achievements linger, and comments posted on Facebook in recent years include the following:

- Fantastic pony … despite his size he saw off all opposition and enthralled millions.
- Met Stroller 'at home' when he had retired. It was around Christmas time and he looked like a typical shaggy Thelwell pony – nothing like an Olympic showjumper.
- My favourite ever showjumper. The Irish-bred pony with the jump of a stag and the heart of a lion.

## 'Our Jimmy'

Close to the play area in Central Park, Peterborough, stands a memorial (restored and rededicated in 2003), the inscription on which reads:

> Our Jimmy, born on the Somme June 1916.
> Mascot of the 1st Scottish Rifles.
> Died 10 May 1943.
> Bought by Mrs Heath in 1920 to give him a good home and to promote interest in the RSPCA.

The epitaph tells only a little of the story of Jimmy the donkey, who is said to have carried ammunition to the troops at the Front and helped transport injured soldiers back to safe quarters. He was wounded by shrapnel no less than three times and, for his bravery, was posthumously awarded the Dickin Medal after his death in 1943.

Military legend has it that Jimmy was foaled on the battlefield after his mother was fatally wounded while she was actually in the process of giving birth – and that 'the Germans ... stopped firing in order to witness the drama, and even cheered as Jimmy was successfully delivered and taken safely back from the frontline'.

Having survived the Somme and all subsequent hostilities, Jimmy was transported to Peterborough; the most likely reason being that his regiment was based there for a time prior to its return to Scotland. Then, in 1920, he was bought by a Mrs Heath who, according to an online article (www.westernfrontassociation.com/world-war-i-articles/don-t-forget-the-war-donkey) gave him a good home and 'used him as the figurehead for a fundraising drive which raised thousands of pounds for charities like the RSPCA'.

Jimmy died (of natural causes) in 1943 and such was his celebrity status, was buried in Central Park and the original memorial erected. In other circumstances, that might well have been the end of the tale but, in the 1970s, the son of a local horse dealer claimed that 'the whole story was a hoax, and his dad had simply sold a donkey to the RSPCA in the 1920s which he had actually bought from a gypsy family and then given a colourful but wholly made-up background.' It's a claim disputed by many – including representatives of the regimental museum of the Scottish Rifles Association, who, from the information they have, are of the opinion that Jimmy's credentials as the working mascot of the 1st Battalion remain bona fide.

## Raise a glass

Every year, on 7 February, glasses are raised to Winston in the clubhouse of Imber Court, a property purchased in 1919 as a training centre for the mounted section of the Metropolitan Police. The glasses raised are not in honour of wartime Prime Minister Winston Churchill but to a chestnut-coloured police horse foaled in 1937 and purchased (and named) by the police in 1944.

While on active police service, Winston was ridden by King George VI at the first Trooping the Colour ceremony to be held after the Second World War on 12 June 1947 and was retired from police (and royal) duties in 1956. Sadly, while being exercised at the police training base, the horse slipped and had to be put down as a result of irreparable injuries. Google research suggests that, in addition to an original photograph of Winston (the horse, not the prime minister!) hanging in the Members' Bar and the annual February toast, a 'memorial to Winston's final resting place can still be found in the grounds of Imber Court'.

## A horse named Vonolel

Tucked away in the grounds of the seventeenth-century Royal Hospital (now home to the Irish Museum of Modern Art) at

Kilmainham, Dublin, a small headstone marks the grave of Vonolel, a horse belonging to British forces' commander, Lord Frederick Roberts.

Purchased in India in 1877 as a four-year-old – and given the name of Vonolel after a Lushai king whose descendants Roberts had done battle with some six years earlier – the horse became something of a hero; so much so that, after being involved in action during the Second Anglo-Afghan War, he was decorated with medals, on the occasion of which, the *Irish Times* mentioned their presentation in the following manner: 'When the Queen [Victoria] awarded medals to her officers and men who had taken part in the Afghan campaign and in the expedition to Kandahar, she did not forget Vonolel. Lord Roberts hung round the animal's neck, the Kabul medal ... and the bronze Kandahar Star.'

Vonolel – said to be a 'white charger of Arabian origin [which] traces his descent from the best blood of the desert' – lived until the age of twenty-nine and was buried in the grounds of the hospital after having been given full military honours, including being saluted with a volley of gunshots over his grave. The headstone is inscribed with the following epitaph:

> There are men both good and wise
> Who hold that in a future state
> Dumb creatures we have cherished here below
> Shall give us joyous greeting when
> We pass the golden gate
> Is it folly that I hope it may be so?

However, not all of Vonolel was buried. In 1904, Lord Roberts commissioned a silver bowl marking the Kandahar expedition and commemorating Vonolel by name. The base of the bowl – now in the possession of the National Army Museum, London – is decorated with his four hooves, polished and silver-tipped.

*Equine Epitaphs*

## A symbolic inclusion

There are many equine memorials throughout the world. Obviously it would be impossible to mention every site but, in much the same way as the Tomb of the Unknown Warrior in Westminster Abbey symbolises all British soldiers who lost their lives in the First World War, it might be relevant to include just one memorial here from overseas as being a typical tribute to all the animals that died in worldwide warfare. The one chosen commemorates the horses of the 7th Cavalry who fought at the Battle of the Little Bighorn, south-central Montana, America – but it could have been one from anywhere that horses have been involved in conflict.

At the Battle of the Little Bighorn, June 1876, the combatants were warriors of the Lakota Sioux, Northern Cheyenne, and Arapaho tribes fighting soldiers of the US Cavalry (famously led by General Custer). Historians have long recorded the reasons for the battle and the names of those who fought but sadly, very little is said of the equine casualties – in fact the burial places of those lost in that particular battle were forgotten until being rediscovered by workmen digging a drainage pipeline in 1941. Archaeological studies took place in 1946 and 2002, and the site has now been credited with a long overdue (and very small) marker stone containing the following words:

In Memory Of
7th Cavalry Horses
Killed During
Custer's Last Stand
June 25, 1876
And Later Buried Here
In July 1881
Under Supervision Of

Lt Charles F. Roe
Of The 2nd Cavalry

A horse named Comanche was the only equine survivor of the Battle of the Little Bighorn. Some two days after Custer's defeat, a burial party came across the severely wounded animal and took him to Fort Lincoln. Having recovered from his injuries, Comanche was subsequently moved to Fort Riley where he was extremely well looked after until his death (ironically, of colic rather than a result of his wounds and trauma suffered in battle) aged twenty-nine. By that time something of a legend to both the soldiers and the general public, officers of the 7th Cavalry decided that Comanche should be preserved for posterity and prevailed upon Lewis Lindsay Dyche of the University of Kansas to mount the remains – which were donated to the university and are, at the time of writing, on display in a humidity-controlled glass case at the university's Museum of Natural History.

## A particularly poignant memorial

Arguably, one of the most poignant memorials to the part horses, donkeys and mules played in the First World War – and to the atrocities they endured – must be the Animals in War memorial, located at Brook Gate, Park Lane, London. While it quite correctly commemorates other animals (and birds – in particular, carrier pigeons) which proved so vital to the 'war effort', it is, in the opinion of many, the depictions of the equines that most affect the visitor.

Unveiled by HRH the Princess Royal in November 2004, the memorial was created by sculptors David Backhouse (responsible for the bronze animals), Richard Holliday and Harry Gray (those depicted in stone) and is constructed in both Portland stone and cast bronze.

# 6

# HORSES IN WAR

Actual contact between man and horse (and domestication of the latter) quite probably occurred in Central Asia but exactly when seems unclear. It is, however, known (via documented evidence) that horses were being ridden in China at least around 4000 BC. Using horses in such a way obviously allowed warriors more mobility and gave them the opportunity to travel further in their bid to explore and conquer new land. The development of spoked wheels and the knowledge and wherewithal to use iron to shoe the wheels – and as axles and other elementary parts – widened the possibilities even further. By literally coupling horses with new technology, it allowed equipment and materials to be transported and for chariots as used by both the Romans and Boadicea (aka Boudica or Boudicca), queen of the ancient British Iceni tribe, to revolutionise warfare as had never before been possible.

## The horse in biblical battle

The *King James Bible* was published in 1611 as a 'modern' English translation of the Bible intended for the Church of England. It's said by some to have influenced the English language and literature more than any other single book. It therefore seems appropriate in this section to include this extract from Job 39:19–25 at the point where God asks Job:

> Have you given the horse strength? Have you clothed his neck with thunder? Can you frighten him like a locust? His majestic snorting strikes terror. He paws in the valley, and rejoices in his strength; he gallops into the clash of arms. He mocks at fear, and is not frightened; nor does he turn back from the sword. The quiver rattles against him, the glittering spear and javelin. He devours the distance with fierceness and rage; nor does he stand firm because the trumpet has sounded. At the blast of the trumpet he says, 'Aha!' He smells the battle from afar, the thunder of captains and shouting.

## A wooden horse for entrance and exit

Legend and mythology have it that, back in history, the Greeks used a large wooden horse in order to gain entry into the city of Troy during the Trojan War. In the Second World War, Eric Williams and other prisoners of war used a very different type of wooden horse – one more usually used as a vaulting box in the gym – under the cover of which they effected a tunnel escape from Stalag Luft III.

## Winning his spurs

In medieval England, the son of a well-to-do family who wished to go into battle or compete in tournaments would be first employed in the somewhat menial role of page boy before graduating to the role of squire. Then, if the squire wanted to become a knight (and most of them did), he had first to acquit himself on the battlefield fighting in the service of his monarch. With his bravado duly proven, he would then be presented with a symbolic pair of spurs and be elevated in the rankings to be given the much sought-after title.

## Medieval horse hierarchy

Popular thinking has it that all horses used in battle – and for jousting – during medieval times were huge, lumbering types. Some certainly needed to be strong enough to carry the weight of a knight in full armour and those that were, are nowadays referred to as being a 'destrier' – a type rather than a specific breed which are said to have been brought to England by William the Conqueror and his army.

Other types also existed – among them a smaller, less well-boned (and faster) animal known as the 'courser'. Ridden by lesser knights and nobility, they were the most-oft used in battles and, although smaller than the destrier, were larger than the third category, the 'rouncey'; the latter described by equine historians as being 'a more general-purpose horse, which could be kept as a riding horse or trained for war' and was 'commonly used by squires, men-at-arms, or poorer knights'.

## Height restrictions apply

War horses were obviously in great demand at a time when there seemed to be innumerable battles going on both in Britain and when England was fighting for land and supremacy abroad. In the early part of the fifteenth century there was even an edict that required the owners of castles and their surrounding estates to keep a certain number of suitable brood mares which were, according to historians, only to be serviced by stallions standing at over 14hh in height. The actual numbers of mares to be kept was dependent on the amount of property and land these landowners had at their disposal. Henry VII apparently forbid the export of any mares 'under three years of age or above a certain value, and stallions of any value'.

## Riding roughshod

For a while during the 1700s, it became commonplace in many countries for cavalry horses to be 'rough-shod' with nails deliberately left proud in order to help the horse have a better foothold in wet, or icy conditions. In battle, if a horse had been rough-shod, not only might it grip the ground better during a cavalry charge, but protruding horseshoe nails or other small, sharp pieces of metal fixed to the shoes by the farrier, could cut and damage horses and soldiers on the opposing side. All well and good in theory but in reality, it was soon found that rough-shod horses could just as easily injure themselves or others of the regiment taking part in the charge and so this somewhat barbaric practice was relatively short-lived.

## A gruesome reminder

During the Trooping the Colour and at other state occasions, at the back of the escort of the Household Cavalry, the Farrier Corporal of Horse can usually be seen carrying what are now, ceremonial axes. The axes did though, at one time, serve a practical, if somewhat gruesome purpose within the cavalry regiments: the spiked part of the axe facilitated the task of putting severely injured horses out of their misery while the sharp blade was used to chop off the hoof of a dead horse in order that the regimental number it carried could be taken back to the quartermaster as proof that a particular animal had actually been killed and not sold on by unscrupulous soldiers.

Slightly less macabre is the other reason for the axe being carried in such situations. On rough unmade roads and over uneven ground, it wasn't unusual for horses pulling vehicles or artillery guns to slip and fall and intelligent use of the axe could quickly free them from the traces and harness in which they had become entangled.

## Horseshoes in heraldry

According to a Lieutenant-Colonel W. L. Julyan writing in *The Field* magazine in 1940, William the Conqueror 'brought farriers with his army ... Henry de Ferres or Ferrers who came over with William ostensibly got his surname from his job as inspector of farriers [and] his descendants bore six horseshoes as part of their arms'. More recent research reveals that Henry de Ferrers was actually Master of Horse to William and that the coat of arms features 'six black horseshoes on a silver background'.

Several other family coats of arms depict horseshoes, not all of which necessarily indicate that there is an obvious connection to the art of shoeing a horse. However, one which most definitely does have direct relevance is that of The Worshipful Company of Farriers. Granted to the Company in September 1968, the following description is exactly as it is included in their website (www.wcf.org.uk/coat-of-arms):

Arms: Argent three Horseshoes on a Bordure Sable with three Nails palewise of the field.

Crest: On a Wreath of the Colours an Arm embowed issuing from Clouds from the sinister side all proper holding in the Hand a Farrier's Hammer Azure hafted and Crowned Or.

Supporters: On either side a Horse Argent gorged with a Collar pendant therefrom a Sword Gules. The red sword suspended from the collar of each supporter refers to the Company's long association with the City of London.

Motto: *VI ET VIRTUTE*: 'By strength and by virtue'.

## For the want of a nail

Many people know – and frequently use – the old adage 'for the want of a nail, a shoe was lost' without necessarily fully understanding its meaning, or even being aware of the full verse which, with a few variations, includes the following lines:

> For want of a nail, the shoe was lost.
> For want of a shoe, the horse was lost.
> For want of a horse, the rider was lost.
> For want of a rider, the battle was lost.
> For want of a battle, the kingdom was lost,
> And all for the want of a horseshoe nail.

In *Poor Richard's Almanac* (1758) Benjamin Franklin included a version – which he preceded with the words: 'A little neglect may breed great mischief'. During the Second World War, it's said that the verse (or something similar to that above) hung on the wall of the Anglo–American Supply Headquarters in London and was intended to remind all who worked there of the importance of keeping abreast of trivial repair parts and inventory replenishment.

Theories as to the origins of the proverb are many: some say it derives from thirteenth-century Germany and the writings of Freidank, whose version, in translation, goes along these lines: 'The wise tell us that a nail keeps a shoe, a shoe keeps a horse, a horse keeps a knight, a knight, who can fight, keeps a castle.' As far as any English mention is concerned, it's believed that the bones of the proverb go back as far as the fourteenth century; others claim it might have been relevant to King Richard III's death during the Battle of Bosworth Field in 1485 and was referred to in William Shakespeare's play, *Richard III*.

## Horsepower

The incredible suffering, injuries and bravery of horses and mules taken to help with warfare on the Western Front and elsewhere during the First World War has already been mentioned (and will be referred to again later) but their role can never be overestimated.

Initially requisitioned from many sources in Britain (in the fortnight after war had been declared some 165,000 horses, ponies and mules were bought by the Army), they were at first mainly intended for use by the cavalry but, as the war years progressed, they were increasingly used as transport enabling military guns, supplies and other paraphernalia to be taken to where they were needed – and, of course, to pull ambulances (both human and equine) to relative safety when the inevitable casualties had occurred.

Even before the outbreak of the conflict the War Office had already begun to identify the types of horses likely to prove useful for military purposes. As early as 1912 the Board of Agriculture and Fisheries produced a booklet entitled *Types of Horses Suitable for Army Remounts* giving details of the variety – and their intended purpose:

- The Household Cavalry: Need black horses of four years 15.3 hands high. At six years 16 hands high.
- Cavalry of the Line: The horse needs deep, short legs, short back, good barrel (of the hunter stamp) light, active and moves easily without brushing of joints. Well ribbed and plenty of bone.
- Royal Artillery: Need weight-carrying hunter. Able to take its place in a gun team in an emergency. At four years 15.2 to 16 hands.

- Royal Engineers and ASC: Draught horses known as 'parcel vanners' able to trot with a good load behind. At four years 15.2 to 15.3 hands.
- Mounted Infantry: Of the cob or Galloway class. Quick, active and gallop short distances. At four years 14.2 to 15.1 hands. May be used in polo.

## Remount and ready

While numbers as to the horses and mules requisitioned by the Army in the UK have been quoted elsewhere, they might be seen as being at odds with any overall totals given – the reason being that, in addition to the ones bred and born in the British Isles, their numbers were supplemented by horses and mules purchased or otherwise acquired from North and South America and mules from Spain and Portugal. All required training – some of them at the remount depots situated around Britain.

Immediately prior to the commencement of the First World War there were five established remount depots: Woolwich, Dublin, Melton Mowbray (which, even to this day, continues to train military working horses, equine instructors and farriers), Arborfield Cross and Godalming. A year later, the number of such depots had increased to forty-two – their purpose being to grade animals as to their suitability (common faults apparently being 'nervous about the head, vicious, dangerous, impossible to handle, unmanageable, jibber, kicker, bad to shoe, nappy, wild') and to train those which passed 'grading' to military standards. It was a huge operation involving several thousand personnel – at the remount depot in Romsey, Hampshire, a blog by Sally Hoult on the National Archives website (https://blog.nationalarchives.gov.uk/making-horses-war-army-remount-service) mentions that there were often more than 4,000 horses and mules in the care of the military there – with sometimes as many as 830 horses being sent to Romsey in a single day. The length of an animal's stay at any of the remount depots varied depending upon their trainability and health (some had suffered in transportation) but was generally anywhere between one and four months.

## In the face of adversity

In war, individual horses had their own characteristics and foibles – earning them the respect of the soldiers and the love of those involved with their welfare. Warrior, the mount of General Jack Seely, was particularly popular with the troops. Riding to see the different regiments and batteries of Canadians whom the General led: 'They all shouted "Warrior", ran up to him, asked if he was all right, crowded round him, officers and men alike; he was, as always, very gracious, but a little aloof.'

Songster – at fourteen years of age and only 15hh in height – was taken to the Front at the start of the war where, what he lacked in youth and size, he more than made up for in character. He was known to untie himself from his peg during heavy shelling then come back to his billet when all became quiet again. Songster knew the sound of the trumpet for water and would take himself off to avail himself of the opportunity for a drink before returning to stand waiting patiently for his nosebag.

Horses such as Warrior and Songster were said by veterinarians in the field to have been better able to cope with the stress of warfare and be less likely to suffer from shell shock than some of the finer-bred animals. The latter were seemingly more prone to panic whereas the former types were calmer – and even learnt how to lie down and take cover at the sound of artillery fire.

## Horse hide of a different kind

In America in 1897, John Sievers Jr. was granted a patent for a duck-shooting hide shaped like a cow. The patent specifications indicated that the hide was to be manufactured using a flexible shell of tanned cow skin, canvas, or similar material and be painted like a typical bovine. The idea was to walk the hide towards a likely spot for waterfowl and then, at the right moment, the hunter concealed within could, through a hinged neck portion, poke out his gun and, as the patent had it, 'discharge his fowling piece'.

In the years before this specific invention, those keen to get close to their intended quarry had developed a similar method to that which Sievers eventually patented but instead of a cow, used a flat life-sized silhouette of a horse, behind which they could hide before taking a shot. Known as a 'stalking horse' (from which the expression of the same name derives), the two ideas were combined and used as a method of concealment by the French army as late in history as the First World War only, rather than a silhouette or cow-skinned hide, they used dummy horses made from papier mâché. Large enough to contain a soldier on observational duties, they weren't an unusual addition to the debris of the battlefield which was, unfortunately, littered with the corpses of many dead equines.

## A picture paints a thousand words

Ernest Brooks was the first official British war photographer to go to the Western Front. Many of his photographs were of the horses involved at Gallipoli and recorded the incredible efforts of the veterinary surgeons involved in trying to treat injured horses and getting them fit enough to return to battle. There was, sadly, much for the veterinary surgeons to do (it's said that 2½ million equines required treatment during the course of the war) but their efforts might possibly have not been sufficiently recognised were it not for the evidence of Brooks' camera. After the war ended in 1918, Ernest Brooks went on to be employed taking photographs of horses undergoing skin disease treatment at the Veterinary Hospital at Neufchâtel, near Etaples – thus adding much to the knowledge of veterinary surgeons then and, through his photographs, those who were to follow in the profession.

## Horsepower upgrade

It seems that while the German and Russian armies of the Second World War were still using a vast number of horses and mules, the British and Allied forces employed them in only a limited fashion (and numbers). Mules were noted for their ability to withstand extremes of weather conditions, particularly if – as with the troops fighting in Italy – they had been requisitioned from local sources and were, therefore, used to the climate and suffered less as a consequence. Italian-bred mules were used to some extent during fighting at the Battle of Monte Cassino as the Allies attempted to facilitate an advance into Rome during the early part of 1944 and, when the Sherwood Rangers Yeomanry regiment were mobilised at the outbreak of war in 1939 and sent to Palestine in early 1940, they were still, in essence, horsed cavalry so took with them animals requisitioned in Britain. In Palestine, riders and their mounts carried out security tasks, and while doing so 'A' Squadron made a mounted charge against rioters and looters in the main street of Haifa – a last task before the horses were finally withdrawn and the regiment converted to mechanical military vehicles.

## Myth versus reality

One of the oft-mentioned myths of the Second World War is that of the seemingly courageous Polish cavalry charging directly at German tanks while mounted on horseback. In reality, at the Battle of Mokra, Polish riders dismounted and, from a distance, used anti-tank weapons to destroy or damage around

100 German tanks and armoured vehicles so it was nowhere near as suicidal a mission as some make out – and certainly one with a lower death toll than that of the poor unfortunate cavalrymen involved in the 'Charge of the Light Brigade' made famous by Alfred, Lord Tennyson.

## Reckless by name but not by nature

In honour of her invaluable service carrying munitions and other essentials during the Korean War (1950–1953) on behalf of the United States Marine Corps, a packhorse named Reckless was awarded two Purple Heart military decorations and earned a salute from almost 2,000 servicemen as they were presented.

## 'We Also Serve'

The People's Dispensary for Sick Animals (PDSA) Dickin Medal – the highest award any animal can receive while serving in military conflict – came into being in 1943 in Britain at the instigation of Maria Dickin who wished to honour the work of animals in the Second World War. A bronze medallion bearing the words 'For Gallantry' and 'We Also Serve' within a laurel wreath (on a ribbon of striped green, dark brown, and pale blue), it is recognised worldwide as being the animal equivalent of the Victoria Cross.

The PDSA website (www.pdsa.org.uk/what-we-do/animal-awards-programme/pdsa-dickin-medal) gives details of three police horses awarded the Dickin Medal during the Second World War:

### Olga

On duty when a flying bomb demolished four houses in Tooting and a plate-glass window crashed immediately in front of her. Olga, after bolting for 100 yards, returned to the scene of the incident and remained on duty with her rider, controlling traffic and assisting rescue organisations.

**Upstart**
While on patrol duty in Bethnal Green a flying bomb exploded within 75 yards, showering both horse and rider with broken glass and debris. Upstart was completely unperturbed and remained quietly on duty with his rider controlling traffic, etc., until the incident had been dealt with.

**Regal**
Was twice in burning stables caused by explosive incendiaries at Muswell Hill. Although receiving minor injuries, being covered by debris and close to the flames, this horse showed no signs of panic.

# 7

# WORKING HORSES

Olga, Upstart and Regal, mentioned at the end of the previous section as being police horses in the streets of London during the bombings of the Second World War were obviously working horses – and brave ones at that. Some of the ones lucky enough to have survived the battlefields of the First World War returned home – and to work. Bill Tull, from Milland, Hampshire, was born in 1920 and spent a lifetime in agriculture. Interviewed for *Milland: Living Memories* compiled by Val Porter (published in 2003), he recalled that, when he left school at fourteen, he went to work on a farm where horses were still used: 'I had the old army horse, Colonel ... we had him until he died ... I worked him on the ploughs and harrows ... Then the poor old horse ... poor old feller, he'd had his chips; they had him done away and bought another one ... He was old; they bought him from the knacker man. Then they bought a tractor.'

Some of the horsemen of old despaired at the arrival of 'new-fangled ideas' at the time when tractors and other agricultural machinery began to take over from the working horse – some, such as Fred Archer (the farmer, author and broadcaster, not the jockey of the same name) foretold, quite rightly, that heavy tractors, combine harvesters and the like would result in 'compacting the soil and damaging its drainage abilities, as well as destroying the fine tilth that years of horse-drawn methods had created.'

In parts of the countryside, horses are once more being employed in a traditional way. Where less impact is required on the soil, winegrowers in France are increasingly using horses to work among the vines. Likewise in the woodlands where horses can ably pull out heavy trunks of timber – thus saving damage that would occur when using tractors and other heavy machinery. They are more fuel efficient too!

## Politically incorrect

Once almost always referred to as the 'Suffolk Punch', the Suffolk horse – as currently defined in the breed standards of the Suffolk Horse Society is, in colour:

> Chesnut [note spelling minus the 't' as chestnut would generally be spelt]. No other colour is allowed. Historically seven shades of chesnut were defined, dark liver, dull dark, light mealy, red, golden, lemon and bright. However, the Society will accept liver, dark, red, light, or bright chesnut … Whole colour is preferred but a certain amount of white on the face is acceptable. A scattering of silver or white hairs on the body is allowed. White to the fetlock is allowed but is regarded as a fault and is not acceptable for stallions being used for breeding. Hoof colour is not prescribed so will be either pigmented or unpigmented.

As to their overall stature, stance and appearance, an old saying, somewhat politically incorrect in this day and age, yet still often used by lovers of the breed, goes something like this: 'The Suffolk has the face of an angel; the body of a beer barrel – and a backside like a farmer's daughter!'

## A gratifying sight
Nineteenth-century writer Charles Apperley (aka 'Nimrod') had this to say on the subject of the men who followed the plough: 'To see a well-grown young Englishman walking between the stilts of his plough with a free step and an erect body, with both horses and plough under his command, is a gratifying sight to a reflecting mind.'

## A financial incentive
Autumn ploughing matches for vintage tractors and horses always draw a regular crowd. Some go for the day out, some to meet old friends. Most though, go to appreciate the power and beauty of the heavy horses which, at the hands of an expert (quite literally) in their field, plough the proverbial straight furrow.

The origins of the ploughing matches were most definitely money-orientated. At a time when those who had always lived and worked on the land began to drift towards urban work in order to earn more money for their family, various rural-based associations attempted to encourage farm workers to stay on the land by holding competitions which offered financial incentives in the way of prizes for excellence in skilled labour and craftsmanship. Sometimes the money offered in such competitions was sufficient to satisfactorily augment the basic ploughman's wage – and, as a winner of a prestigious match, might even lead to better employment. It would certainly create pride in one's work due to the fact that creating a good furrow was considered to be the ultimate test of agricultural skill – and likely to make the victor the envy of local horsemen.

## Have horse, will travel
Bill Tull (mentioned in the introductory paragraph of this particular section) said that, after his father came home from the First World War, 'he used to breed mares and foals ... for Mr Lamb at Borden

Wood and did a lot of show work with shires.' One of the show horses was a stallion named Rock (or possibly Rocky) who was a frequent prize-winner and was, therefore, in great demand as a sire. A part of Bill's father's work involved walking Rock (and other 'travelling stallions' from the farm) to service mares over a wide distance, often taking up much of the week – and no doubt tiring Mr Tull with the miles he covered walking and the stallion by the mares he covered while fulfilling his duties at stud!

## A regular delivery

In towns and cities, alongside the many and varied delivery vans, public transport of the time was mainly horse-drawn. The omnibus (meaning 'for all' in its Latin context) system in London in the 1890s was operated by some 25,000 horses pulling 2,000 buses on the roads of the capital. Research (unsubstantiated) suggests that 'The last London horse bus ran on 4 August 1914, the day Britain declared war on Germany.'

For several years after the Second World War, some villages still depended upon a horse and cart to transport and empty toilet buckets from the outside 'privy'. Slightly more glamorous was the role of the horse or pony who delivered the daily milk. The Co-operative Wholesale Society (originating in 1844 in Rochdale, Lancashire) had, in 1919, 6,000 horse-drawn vehicles delivering both milk and other groceries on its behalf.

## No use crying over spilt milk

A news item in the 1 October 1936 edition of the *Wallington and Carshalton Times* was headlined 'Bolting Horse Leaves Trail of Milk' and went on to describe the incident in a quite alarming manner:

> Startled by the backfiring of a motor car in Green Lane, St Helier, on Tuesday morning, a horse drawing a milk cart bolted. Small

children playing on the grass strip in the middle of the road scattered in terror and their shrieks brought tenants of the homes to their doors in alarm.

Opposite the entrance to Legion Court, the horse swerved on to the grass strip. The wheels of the cart struck the kerb with such force that it was overturned, dragging the frightened animal to the ground.

The roundsman in charge had been delivering orders at the time of the backfire but as soon as his attention was attracted to the runaway horse he gave chase and reached the spot in time to prevent the horse resuming its escape.

The crash of milk bottles as the cart overturned was heard hundreds of yards away and a large crowd gathered to witness the roundsman's efforts to pacify the horse and attend to its minor cuts and bruises.

More than sixty pints of milk were splashed over the road. As the bottles broke fragments of glass flew through the air, some being found fifteen yards away. Dozens of eggs suffered multiple fractures and yolks mingled with the spilt milk to give a portion of Green Lane another colour. One or two bottles of milk were, however, undamaged.

## Boats and trains

For more than 250 years horses were used to move goods to and from Liverpool Docks. At their peak it's estimated that in excess of 20,000 worked both on the streets and in the docks – apart from London, that's more horses than in any other city in the British Isles. In 2010, to commemorate their importance in commerce, equine sculptor Judy Boyt was commissioned to produce *Waiting*, a statue of a Liverpool dock horse standing patiently ready to pull its next load – at the base of which reads the inscription: 'If it came in, we shifted it.'

Almost a century and a half after the first passenger train ran from Stockton to Darlington, heavy horses were still proving useful to the railway companies and continued to be in demand in some rail yards as a means of moving train carriages from one line to another – a procedure known as 'shunting'. Along with Dr Richard Beeching's closure of many branch line stations in the mid-1960s, in 1967 Charlie the Clydesdale was retired from work in the Newmarket Station shunting yard – and, with his departure, the British railway system ended its association with the working horse.

According to Susanna Forrest writing in her amazingly well-researched book, *The Age of the Horse* (Atlantic Books, 2016), on the canals and waterways, the horses which began pulling the barges at the dawn of the Industrial Revolution were not, at first, the heavy shire types one might expect but were instead, 'lighter draughts, or even ponies or donkeys'. The weight the larger animals could pull over water as opposed to their ability on land was phenomenal: Susanna Forrest cites the fact that 'two canal horses could … draw fifty to eighty short tons – fifty to eighty times what two wagon horses could manage [on the road].'

## Have a drink on me

In 1859, in consideration of the fact that many of the poorer dwellings in London had no access to running water, the Metropolitan Drinking Fountain Association was set up by Samuel Gurney, MP and philanthropist, and barrister Edward Thomas Wakefield to provide free drinking water for people – and added 'and Cattle Trough' to its name in 1867 in the hope of improving animal welfare; in particular, that of the vast numbers of horses working on the streets of the capital.

As the Metropolitan Drinking Fountain and Cattle Trough Association, its president was the then Duke of Westminster and its offices were situated in Victoria Street, Westminster. Supported entirely by voluntary contributions, requests for bequests pointed out that the association was 'the only agency for providing free supplies of water for man and beast in the streets of London and the relief it affords, both to human beings and dumb animals, is incalculable'. Their advertising further pointed out that

> The total number of troughs and fountains now erected and at work in the Metropolis, is as follows: – five hundred and ninety-seven troughs for animals, and five hundred and seventy-five fountains for human beings, at which multitudes of men, women and children, horses, oxen, sheep and dogs quench their thirst daily, amounting in aggregate to probably not less than the enormous total of 250,000,000 drinkers in a year.
>
> All the fountains and troughs require constant care and supervision, and are regularly inspected, cleaned, kept in repair, and well supplied with water by the agents of the Society. Half an hour spent at one of them during the heat of the summer would do more to secure sympathy and support for the Association than any words which the committee can use ... Contributions are earnestly solicited ...

Although obviously well intentioned and vital, one cannot help but wonder about the disease implications of having so many animals drinking from a single trough.

## Make hay while the sun shines

Nowadays known as a place of hotels, entertainment and theatre venues, the Haymarket in London existed as far back as the Elizabethan period and was, as its name suggests, a venue for the sale of hay, animal fodder and produce. It was where many of the horsemen of the capital would have bought all that was necessary for the upkeep of the equines used to work the streets of London and its environs.

Although initially a free market, during the lifetime of William III (1650–1702) horse-drawn wagons bringing in the hay and cereals were levied a tax. According to John Timbs, writing in 1855, each was charged at the rate of '3d each load of hay and 2d for straw'. Again according to Timbs, 'The market for hay was removed by Act of Parliament, in 1830, to Cumberland Market, Regent's Park.'

## Well fed and groomed

Some horses working in the towns and cities were poorly treated – but others were extremely well cared for. In *The Horse World of London* (1893), J. W. Gordon informs his readers:

> At Lett's Wharf the [feed] mixture consists of one truss each of hay and straw to three of clover and half a dozen bushels of oats; and of this each horse has forty pounds a day. He has his breakfast at three o'clock in the morning, and takes out a nosebag with him on each journey; sometimes he has a feed of beans or some special mixture; and invariably he has a bran mash to wind up the week with on Saturday night. When he comes in wet and dirty a bale of peat moss is broken for him to stand in, and in this he is thoroughly groomed before he goes to the stable; and he goes to the stall at the word of command, knowing his place quite as well as the horse-keeper. And if he is a City horse, his stall is roomy and lofty ... although he stands not on straw, but on the more economical peat. He lives in good condition ... and he rarely comes to grief in the streets, owing to his driver being by his side to warn him when the paving changes, and check him generally.

## Rag-and-bone man

At the time of writing, if you were to Google 'rag and bone man', very likely the first thing to appear on screen would be the website and information appertaining to English singer Rory Graham, known professionally as Rag 'n' Bone Man. That to one side, long gone are the sights and sounds of the more traditional rag-and-bone man with his horse and cart (shades of television's *Steptoe & Son* – of which more later) on the city streets.

In London, up until the mid-1960s, over thirty 'totters' kept their horses at Norland Gardens, Hammersmith – from where they would each travel out on their individual daily rounds – but then, in order to make way for new roadworks, the Greater London Council converted garages in Latimer Road, Shepherd's Bush, into stables. As the profession of rag-and-bone man slowly disappeared, so too did the horses and eventually, their stables. Latimer Road is now quite upmarket – although there remain parts that the old rag-and-bone men (and their horses) would still no doubt recognise.

## 'Young Steptoes' – and old problems

In May 2016, some serious fly-tipping by 'young Steptoes' using 'a horse and cart' was, according to West Midlands councillor Peter Smith, 'becoming a major issue in Blakenall ... Much to the annoyance and frustration not only of council officials but local residents, we are having to put up with the antisocial fly-tipping exploits of these modern-day young Steptoes.'

Fly-tipping with a horse and cart is, however, no new thing. According to author Lisa Woollett, in the mid-1800s, many 'master scavengers' ran a profitable business collecting rubbish from the 'dust-holes' of householders. The house owner would be charged for their services and, after sorting and sifting through what had been collected for anything of value (scrap or otherwise), what was left was taken to a designated tip. With profits to be made, their rounds attracted rogue collectors who would undercut the prices of those operating legitimately. In her book *Rag and Bone: A Family History of What We've Thrown Away* (John Murray, 2020), Lisa mentions that 'With no connection to a dust-yard, after sifting for anything of value, they would then dump the remaining ... on a quiet road...'

## In the pit of the earth

Mining for coal to fuel the household fires and those of industry was a dangerous and dirty job for the humans employed to hew it from the underground stratum. It was no less so for the small pit ponies (generally Shetlands no more than 12hh high) which, working an average of an eight-hour shift, were used to haul wagons of coal along narrow rail tracks from the coalface to a point from where it could be lifted to the surface. It was a system first begun in the mid-eighteenth century and continued until virtually the mid-twentieth century. (It's thought that in 1999, two pit ponies working in a small, private drift mine in South Wales were the very last in Britain to be retired.)

In the mid-1800s, records have it that some 200,000 ponies (and the occasional horse) were being used in the UK mining industry, most of whom were stabled underground and only ever came to the surface once a year when the collieries shut down for the annual holidays. The work wasn't solely confined to underground – horses more substantial than the average pit pony were used to operate winding gear to either bring coal to the surface or, in mines where water and flooding was a problem, to turn wheels in a kind of pumping system which brought up water from the mine shafts in order to prevent them from becoming waterlogged and unworkable.

## Beside the seaside and on the streets

Although it was more usual to use ponies, donkeys were sometimes employed at the mines during Victorian times. More commonly, however, they were used by traders to make deliveries due to the fact that they were cheaper and easier to keep than horses and ponies. In Ireland, they transported peat cut for fuel. On the coast, donkeys pulled carts and carried panniers collecting cockles, mussels and seaweed but, as the railway system improved and trains began taking holidaymakers for a day trip to the seaside, the donkey owners there quickly latched on to the idea that they could supplement their earnings by offering donkey rides to the tourists – and thus a brand-new holiday entertainment was born.

In general, donkeys tended not to be well treated and there are many newspaper reports of the time telling of owners being taken to court and fined (or even jailed) for cruelty. The Earl of Shaftesbury, well known for his campaigning against child labour, was equally as diligent in trying to improve the lives of donkeys being worked by the costermongers of the cities and towns. Some had previously rented both barrows and donkeys to pull them and Shaftesbury began a scheme whereby the costermongers could, through a special purchase scheme, buy their own animals – and, in order to encourage them to take better care of them, had the idea of donkey shows, the first of which took place in 1874.

## An unusual guard dog

Donkeys can be trained to do useful tasks. As to their versatility in other circumstances, in April 2021 viewers of BBC Television's *Countryfile* were introduced to Katie, a teenager farming with her parents in Cumbria. In the piece, Katie mentioned that, during lambing time, the family donkey was grazed with the sheep as doing so kept the foxes away. Nik Smith, a donkey owner with a great deal of experience, helps to explain why: 'They, like horses, are prey animals but do not possess the speed or lung capacity to outrun a predator that a horse does. When spooked, a horse will run 500 metres before stopping. A donkey will run five, then turn and face the problem before deciding what to do. Donkeys are more likely to fight than flee.'

In many parts of rural America, cattle farmers graze a donkey or mule in the pasture in order to keep coyotes and wolves away. As one rancher mentions: 'They are tough and have great eyesight and intelligence. I've heard of donkeys kicking the crap out of coyotes ...'

## A stubborn streak

In March 2024, during an episode of BBC Radio 4's excellent *Ramblings* series hosted by Clare Balding, Hannah Engelkamp told Clare of her extraordinary adventure walking 1,000 miles around the perimeter of Wales with her donkey Chico. It was a journey Hannah undertook without any previous experience of 'donkeys or horses, or any animals really' and was much harder than she ever imagined. As Hannah explained to Clare and her radio listeners, the oft-held thinking of 'carrot or stick' didn't work and one of the first things she learnt on the trip was that 'when a donkey stops you just have to wait and stand and look and wait until the moment seems right to move off again'.

There are several accounts of Queen Victoria and her children using various donkeys to pull them in carriages around the grounds of the royal estates. One particular carriage and somewhat characterful-sounding donkey is mentioned in an 1893 issue of *The Idler* magazine:

> This vehicle is much used by Her Majesty when driving about the grounds, and is drawn by an exceedingly strong, handsome donkey

called 'Jacquot', in colour a very dark brown, with white nose and curiously knotted tail. 'Jacquot' ... is a very intelligent animal, with a rather strong objection to work, and a great love of good living ...

## All the Queen's horses

Although living in grand style, the horses stabled at Windsor could, nevertheless, be referred to as being 'working horses' due to the fact that many of them are employed in pulling the carriages for state occasions. In Scotland, at Balmoral, the late Queen Elizabeth II had a stable of Highland ponies, the history of which can be traced back centuries – perhaps even to the time of the Vikings' arrival in the latter part of the ninth century. After her death in 2022, Elizabeth's Highland ponies were moved elsewhere and, at the time of writing, only four remain at Balmoral where they undertake traditional duties around the estate. The late queen wasn't the first monarch to have kept that type of pony at her Scottish residence and it's said that, in addition to their everyday tasks in the hills, Queen Victoria used them as riding ponies, particularly when accompanied by her servant and almost constant companion in later life, John Brown.

Highland ponies were (and continue to be) used by the gillies employed on many Scottish estates in order to bring shot deer down from the hills after a successful stalking foray and to carry panniers to and from the grouse moors. Their training is interesting: to accustom them to the smell of a dead and sometimes bloody deer carcass, young ponies are sometimes fed on and around a fresh deer skin and, to accustom them to the feel of the panniers carried either side of their body, full hay nets are tied in front of the saddle area with the panniers behind – the idea being that the young horse, when turning round to investigate, would find only sweet-smelling hay. As they are led, the hay nets get them used to both carrying a load wider than a saddle and also the sound of the creaking panniers – usually made of wicker.

Occasionally an example of a Highland pony being worked on the hills is referred to as a 'garran' (or 'garron') as if it might be a different, distinct breed but, in the Scottish Gaelic language, the word loosely translates as being a generic term for a gelding or any small, sturdy horse of working ability.

## 'A wretched load of crocks'

Working horses, ponies and pack-mules were frequently used by explorers worldwide in order to transport equipment and supplies. Although all their work would have been arduous over wild terrain with no existing tracks or pathways, for a very unfortunate few, the going was more arduous than most.

Captain Robert Falcon Scott and Lawrence Oates will be forever known for their ill-fated *Terra Nova* Expedition to the South Pole. Initially, Oates' role was to look after the ponies which the team hoped to use for sledge-hauling during the journey but the selection of Manchurian ponies purchased ahead of the trip apparently left much to be desired. In November 1910, Oates observed that he was 'not impressed with the ponies. They are very old for a job of this sort. A wretched load of crocks. However, we shall have to make the most of them.'

Almost a year later, at the end of October 1911, three parties left Cape Evans with tractors, sled-dog teams and ten ponies. The first phase of the trip – a distance of some 400 miles – was to reach the base of the Beardmore Glacier. On 12 November, Scott notes: 'I am anxious about these beasts [the ponies] ... and if they pull through well, all will be thanks to Oates.' However, just six days later, Scott was beginning to have doubts about the suitability of the ponies for their enormous task – as Oates wrote, 'Scott realises now what awful cripples our ponies are.'

On 28 November, one of them, a pony named Chinaman (who Oates said '... must have been a goodish kind of pony fifteen years ago'), was shot, sadly followed on 2 December by both Oates' own pony Christopher and another named Victor ('Good old Victor! He always had a biscuit out of my ration, and he ate his last before the bullet sent him to his rest.') By 9 December, the remaining ponies were gone, much to the apparent relief of Captain Scott: 'I have had more than enough of this cruelty to animals.'

# 8

# EQUINE ARTISTS

From Stubbs to Munnings, from Edgar Degas to Rosa Bonheur, there have been many celebrated 'horse artists' – and the various styles of their work are quite extraordinary. As well as the old traditionalists such as John Frederick Herring Snr, there are many examples of modern-day artists who depict horses in a striking and most accurate manner.

## Six of the best

In the first half of the twentieth century, it was almost impossible to move without stumbling over an equine artist of renown! It being the time it was, several of them had been involved in the First World War, either working in the various remount depots situated throughout Britain or as war artists at the front line. On occasion, both situations applied. As one of them commented in later life, it was 'four solid years of nothing but horse'.

All had a love and understanding of horses, their likely temperament, how they moved and how they worked. It was a knowledge gained from being totally immersed in equine matters whether on the battlefield, hunting field, polo field or racecourse. Some, like Cecil Aldin (see below) even studied animal anatomy at a technical level.

**G. D. Armour** (George Denholm) was born in 1864 and died in 1949 and, in a life well lived, painted and illustrated many books – some of the latter of which contained humorous line drawings that showed off not only his artistic know-how, but also his ability to see the funny side of many experiences noted in the field and countryside. Even out hunting, Armour carried a sketchbook in which he scribbled down various occurrences as they appeared and, as a measure of his love of horses, he at one time converted half of his studio into a stable, the better to observe his subject.

**Lionel Edwards** (1878–1966) is well known for his hunting scenes – and for those of the racecourse. During the First World War he painted dramatic and graphic artwork depicting various cavalry regiments on active duty. Like his contemporaries Armour, Cecil Aldin and Charlie Johnson Payne (of whom more shortly), as well as the paintings for which he is so readily recognised, Edwards also provided sporting illustrations for magazines such as *Country Life* and *Punch* and, alongside many other books, was commissioned to supply illustrations for certain editions of *Black Beauty*.

**Cecil Aldin** (1870–1935) found lucrative work as an illustrator for *The London Illustrated Times* – and also provided artwork for editions of Charles Dickens's *The Pickwick Papers* and *The Jungle Book* by Rudyard Kipling. Many of his (sometimes rather saccharin) depictions of dogs – in particular small ones such as terriers – can still be regularly seen in the form of popular prints or as greetings cards. They are, however, a world apart from his oil paintings of racing, hunting and the English countryside.

**Charlie Johnson Payne** (1884–1967) is arguably better known as 'Snaffles' – whose subject matter was almost always either equestrian (hunting, racing and polo) or military in nature. Many of his paintings (for example, *Once Upon a Time* and *That Far, Far-away Echo*) evocatively incorporate both. One of this particular artist's notable characteristics was to add small pencil drawings, remarques and/or comments and observations either alongside the main picture or on the surrounding mount. He was no different to those artists mentioned previously in that, as well as his commissioned paintings, Johnson Payne helped augment his bank balance by contributing illustrations to periodicals such as *The Bystander* and *The Illustrated Sporting and Dramatic News*.

**Lucy Kemp-Welsh** (1869–1958) was that most rare thing of the time – a recognised female artist, and an extremely successful one at that. Rare in that she made it in a predominantly man's world of art, even more so was the fact that, although unsuccessful in her attempts to gain experience of the First World War at first-hand, she nevertheless got to paint the military while the troops were in training. Time spent with the Royal Horse Artillery on Salisbury Plain resulted in her painting *Forward the Guns!* and undertaking a commission at the Wiltshire-based remount depot on behalf of the Imperial War Museum. Perhaps her biggest achievement, however – most certainly if size has anything to do with it – was her pre-First World War painting entitled *Colt Hunting in the New Forest*, an area she knew well from childhood. That particular painting was exhibited at the Royal Academy before being bought and donated to the Tate Gallery. Like others mentioned here, Lucy's smaller works provided illustrations for several books.

**(Sir) Alfred Munnings** (1878–1959) was, to many people, the most famous artist of this particular era. Rejected by the military due to being blind in his right eye as a result of an accident in his early twenties (a disability that makes his success as an artist even more remarkable) Munnings instead worked as a strapper/groom for remounts at Calcot Park, near Reading, at the commencement of the First World War. It was there that his drawings and paintings of army life came to the attention of Paul Knody, an art critic who had been tasked with finding potential war artists – as a result of which Munnings was taken on by the Canadian army in France. There, General Jack Seely, who, in 1934, wrote *My Horse Warrior* – on which the book, stage play and film *War Horse* is based – became friends with Munnings. Seely described the occasion when the two of them first met:

> He turned up one morning in plain clothes, in this bleak area, where for months no human had been seen in anything but French, English or German uniform. Of course it had never been the intention of the Canadian authorities that Munnings should join us in the front line, but this whimsical and gallant soul thought that this was just the best place to be. And so it turned out, for by common consent his paintings and drawings of the Canadian horses, close up against the front line, are some of the most brilliant things he has ever done.

## The home of an artist

If, like General Seely, you happen to be an admirer of the artwork of Sir Alfred Munnings, one can do no better than visit his home at Castle House at Dedham, on the borders of Suffolk and Essex. Here you can really get the feel of the man by seeing his studio and looking at many of his paintings and working sketches displayed on the walls. The house itself still has very much the feel of a home rather than a museum and, were Munnings able to return from the afterlife, he would no doubt immediately recognise many of the personal possessions and items of furniture.

Photographs of Alfred and his second wife Violet are prominent and in a couple of them, it's possible to see just where they were positioned on the staircase and, should you be of such a mind, to quite literally stand in their footsteps.

## An appreciation of George Stubbs – by Sir Alfred Munnings

Despite his own brilliance at portraying horses, Sir Alfred Munnings readily described himself as being an admirer of the genius and artistic skills of George Stubbs (1724-1806). Rare it is that one can find an appreciation of one artist penned by another but, in an article for *The Horseman's Year* of 1946-1947, Munnings felt moved to write:

> Stubbs at his greatest has caused such a feeling in many of us seeing one of those masterpieces of his hand and eye ... As an Art Student at Norwich, I bought at a second-hand bookseller's an original folio edition of [Stubbs'] *The Anatomy of the Horse*. The most unique thing of its kind ever compiled, this heroic effort, an epic of the eighteenth century, is as great and unselfish a work as anything could be ... we as a nation should be proud of it ...
>
> [Stubbs broke] through the style of painting the horse, not as seen, but as shown on canvas for a hundred years; stiff, unreal, absurd, such as those depicted by Wooton and Seymour, in what we must call large decorative pieces of the Chase and the Turf, which, in gorgeous carved and gilded frames, turned many a wall in hall and staircase, in many a mansion, to splendour ...
>
> It was from this fashion of painting in horse portraiture that Stubbs was to break away; a fashion which satisfied owners who lived hard and drank hard, and cared little about art ... [Of Stubbs' representation of Bay Malton with the jockey, Singleton, against the sky] who can fault this picture? ... That extraordinary bloom

with light in the shadows is magic ... the lighting of the horse is right ... even more, the character is studied and shown to the life; and Stubbs' humour is there in force, showing a great combination of horse and rider, both to live on as long as the canvas lasts.

*Temper tantrums*
Arguably one of Stubbs' best-known paintings is the life-size portrait of Whistlejacket, a racehorse bred in 1749 by Sir William Middleton and later sold to Charles Watson-Wentworth, the second Marquess of Rockingham. Whistlejacket is described as having 'a nearly ungovernable temper' and while Stubbs was standing back the better to critically inspect what he had painted, Simon Cobb, the stable groom who had been holding the horse led him around in order to keep him calm and thereby less likely to fidget. Catching sight of his likeness, it is said that Whistlejacket thought it real enough to cause him to rear and strike at it.

## Fame and Fortunio!
Fortunio Matania, an Italian artist born in 1881, was more interested in depicting historical works than he was in horses. Despite that, he is nevertheless of considerable significance when it comes to portraying the importance of horses and mules during the First World War.

His original of *Last Absolution of the Munsters at Rue du Bois* was destroyed during the bombing of London in the Second World War: the image does, however, still exist online – as does that of *British Trooper Meets French Woman on the Road to Lille* which shows a British trooper and his horse stopping to talk to a woman who, according to the artist's notes, had lost her husband at Verdun. Another of Matania's paintings of the time is *At an Advanced Dressing Station on the Western Front* showing a horse-drawn Red Cross ambulance delivering casualties to a dressing station. Arguably this artist's best-known work is *Goodbye Old Man* illustrating the tremendous bond that existed between First World War soldiers and their horses. Often accompanying the painting whenever it is shown in the media are the words of the poem 'A Soldier's Kiss', by Henry Chappell.

## A picture of bucolic provincialism

So picturesque is the rural scene in which draught horses played a crucial part that even artists more famous for depicting other topics were (and are) frequently tempted to capture the bygone era when the sun seemingly always shone, and harvest picnics took place in the shaded lee of the wagon while the farm horse munched contentedly on the oats in his nosebag.

The late David Shepherd, best known for his paintings of African wildlife and steam engines, was one such artist. A surprising amount of his work depicts shires and farm horses of a bygone era. *Spring Ploughing* features two at work and was inspired by A. E. Housman's poem 'A Shropshire Lad'. Shires also appear in his *Shires on Holiday*, a painting commissioned by Whitbread Breweries which shows galloping 'off-duty' dray horses, and again in *The Old Forge* – where one is having new shoes fitted by the farrier. *The Lunch Break* depicts both man and horse in the 1920s while *Somerset Harvest* evocatively portrays both the hard work and romance of the harvest fields during the same era.

## The world of Thelwell, Penelope and Kipper

Known to many are the cartoons of Norman Thelwell – his portrayal of the pony-obsessed Penelope, her often delinquent mount Kipper and the antics of all their friends have long been perfectly and very amusingly illustrated in books.

Thelwell had his first cartoon published in *Punch* magazine in 1952 and his first pony cartoon was published in 1953. This, by complete accident, led to a lifetime of drawing similar images for newspapers – perhaps most notably, the *Daily Express*. As the artist wrote in his 1986 autobiography, *Wrestling with a Pencil*: 'One day I did a pony drawing and … the response was instantaneous. People telephoned the editor and asked for more. Suddenly I had fan mail. So the editor told me to do a two-page spread on ponies. I was appalled. I thought I'd already squeezed the subject dry. I looked at the white drawing block and wondered what on earth to do. In the end I dreamed up some more horsey ideas and people went into raptures.'

Not realised by many is the fact that, aside from the exploits of Penelope, her riding pals and their precocious ponies, there was also a serious side to Thelwell's art and he was an extremely proficient landscape painter using both watercolour and oils in order to depict atmospheric scenes of the countryside and river near his home in Hampshire.

## Painting perfection

Although Salvador Dali once told fellow artists to 'have no fear of perfection, you'll never reach it', there are many living artists specialising in equine subject matter who, to look at their work, have very definitely achieved perfection. They, though, would probably never admit it for there is, in most artists, no matter what generation, a degree of insecurity and shyness.

Shyness and creativity often go hand in hand. There's frequently a common connection between the deep feeling and introspection that leads to great art – and perhaps that is why, when asked to discuss some of the reasons they paint horses and the feelings that doing so engenders, those approached in connection with *The Horse Lover's Miscellany*, were at first keen to do so, but very little was ultimately forthcoming. On the other hand, possibly their studios were so full of commissions needing completion that they just didn't have the time! Whatever the reason – as a very brief trawl through the internet search engines, social media or a wander around the stands of country fairs and agricultural shows will prove – the absence of mention of any modern-day artists in this section is certainly no reflection on the numbers of those who paint all manner of horse-related topics to perfection.

## Sculptural masterpieces

Not all equine artists work in watercolour, oils, pastels, charcoal or other mediums – some sculpt in stone, wood, with welded metal, clay or in plaster and cast in bronze. Elizabeth Frink was one such person. Fascinated by naturalistic form, including the human body, birds and animals, Frink's *Horse and Rider* (completed in 1974) combines two of these subjects and, as the artist herself described it, is 'an ageless symbol of man and horse'. Londoners and visitors to the capital might have originally seen it at the junction of Piccadilly and Dover Street but when, in 2016, that site was being redeveloped, it was moved to its current position by Old Bond Street. Anyone who has seen it there and then gone to Winchester and walked up to the top end of the High Street might well blink and think they are seeing double as, in front of the court buildings, stands a second cast of the same statue. To confuse matters even further, one of Frink's earliest sculptures (undertaken in 1950 when she was still studying at the Chelsea School of Art) was also given the title *Horse and Rider*!

Had our hypothetical traveller then driven past Hollycombe House near Liphook, Hampshire, when it was the home of the late Tim Hoare and immediately gone on to drive a few miles further towards The Trundle, near Goodwood, they might also have had cause to do a double-take as, in both the grounds of Hollycombe and at The Trundle, identical, much larger than life horses' heads would have most definitely have caught their eye. Both were the work of Nic Fiddian-Green, a contemporary sculptor. As Jay Merrick, writing for *The Independent* mentions: 'These heads have a sentient, alert quality, as if they know we're watching them ... and yet they also radiate an aura of calm.' Fiddian-Green's *Horse at Water* is located at Hyde Park Corner and *Copenhagen: The Iron Duke's Faithful Horse* in the grounds of Wellington College, Berkshire – the latter being donated to the college by 'the families of the leavers of 2012' in honour of the college's 150th anniversary.

If you visit Sculptures by the Lakes in Dorset (the home and workplace of Simon and Monique Gudgeon), among the many sculptures to be seen in glorious outdoor settings is *Brewers Horse* by Gloucestershire-based Gill Parker. On a plinth, it is a much smaller head than any which might come from the studio of Nic Fiddian-Green but what it lacks in size, it more than makes up for in detail and beauty. Gill certainly understands her equine subjects; a keen and knowledgeable horsewoman, she particularly loves to make sculptures appertaining to polo as the game offers 'the movement and athleticism' she likes to portray. Not that that prevents her covering any other horse-related sport and one of her many major commissions was the life-size bronze of Motivator – a thoroughbred racehorse – which stands proudly at Ascot Racecourse.

Also living in Gloucestershire is the artist Rupert Till who specialises in wire sculptures. As Rupert says, 'the wire is my pencil line!' In 2019, he created *Cruising* – a life-size image of a horse and rider jumping over a hedge. In the same year, Rupert completed a private commission in bronze wire for the Close House Golf Club in Newcastle which featured (again life-size) the racehorse Inglis Drever who won at Cheltenham on three occasions.

Sculptor (and portrait artist) Amy Goodman has every reason to be proud of her life-sized *Romsey War Horse* on display at the memorial gardens in the town. Depicting a First World War horse and soldier, it's a poignant reminder to any who need it, of the sufferings and hardships of both animals and humans who, by either choice or conscription, became embroiled in the mud and terror of early twentieth-century battle.

## The horse in art and photography

In *Horse Play: A Necessary Book on the Lighter Side of Riding* (undated but circa 1945), author and illustrator Rowland Hilder explained how cameras were used to reveal the true leg positions of a horse at the gallop:

> It was generally believed ... that the horse galloped along on perpetually outstretched legs; he was depicted thus in all old prints and paintings.
>
> The theory was, however, exploded in about 1872 by Eadweard Muybridge (whose real name was James Edward Muggeridge) [who] invented a way of taking motion pictures; the first pictures to be taken created an international sensation; they were photographs of a moving horse, which showed conclusively that a horse had more than one position in the gallop. Muybridge couldn't quite see what it was, so he tried the camera on a bull – but that didn't help. He made another attempt at photographing horses in 1883, using forty cameras operated by a succession of strings which were pulled by the horses. A series of locomotion pictures were thus produced ... The photographs were recomposed into the original movement by means of different kinds of apparatus ... The upshot of all this was that the horse was found to have two positions in the gallop. This discovery ... altered art considerably.

# 9

# HORSES ON SCREEN

When publishing her research papers entitled *Horse-breakers, Tamers and Trainers: An Historical, Psychological Review* in 1986, Sharon E. Cregier of the University of Prince Edward Island recorded that 'For ninety-eight percent of the last 6,000 years ... the horse was the fastest vehicle available to man. As such, it was easily associated with virtually anything, however unrelated ... for most of us, no other creature combines grace, streamlining, intelligence, and tractability ... The horse is at once powerful, practical, and beautiful.'

Reading Cregier's erudite words and considering just how the horse has given civilisation an means of transportation, power and strength to work the land; a platform from which to fight battles, companionship and yes, even food, it is surely not surprising that horses, ponies, donkeys and mules feature so heavily in films, television dramas, on-screen Saturday afternoon sport, televised coverage of royal weddings, funerals, Trooping the Colour and even in documentaries about horses themselves. On *Netflix*, for example, there are 'true-life' stories about horses and riders preparing for success in the showjumping and eventing world, while the beautifully filmed *My Heroes Were Cowboys* (2021) tells how, after a difficult childhood, Robin

Wiltshire has enjoyed a productive adult life training horses for the big screen.

## Children's television – how the years define us!

Children fortunate enough to have had access to a television in the 1950s and early 1960s might well have watched (in black and white, of course!) *The Adventures of Champion* the 'wonder horse', a wild stallion who befriended twelve-year-old Ricky North in the American Southwest during the 1880s. Alternatively they could have enjoyed the exploits of *The Lone Ranger*, his horse Silver ('Hi-ho, Silver! Away!') and his Native American partner Tonto who rode a horse named Scout. If programmes set in the 'Wild West' were not their thing, there was always Mr Ed the 'talking horse' – recently described online as being a 'half-hour sitcom [that] brought lightness and laughter into every home that was fortunate enough to be able to tune in'. All three were American television series which were ultimately screened in the UK and aired on either BBC or ITV (the only television channels at the time), but that's not to say British producers didn't create any home-grown horse-based series for children – not a bit of it!

In the early 1970s, London Weekend Television (LWT) began showing *The Adventures of Black Beauty* as Sunday tea-time viewing. While it had little real connection to Anna Sewell's book of the same name, it nevertheless proved to be a favourite with both children and their parents. Filmed on location in the Hertfordshire countryside (but set in eighteenth-century Yorkshire), the storyline involved a widowed country doctor and his young family – plus of course, the eponymous hero which, with an obviously higher IQ than most equines, was instrumental in bringing all the weekly adventures to a successful conclusion. A later series (in the 1990s) was, somewhat unimaginatively entitled *The New Adventures of Black Beauty*.

Children watching ITV could also take pleasure from *Follyfoot*, a series which first aired around the same time as *The Adventures of Black Beauty*, and again in the late 1980s. The plotline is based on a girl sent to stay with her uncle on his farm while her parents travel overseas for a year – from where she visits Follyfoot Farm, an establishment that cares for unwanted and unloved horses. Produced by Yorkshire Television in conjunction with a German independent television company who intended to show the series on the ZDF channel, there are similarities in that, in the 1960s, *The White Horses* (following the adventures of a girl, her uncle, his stud groom and Lipizzaner horses) was co-produced by what was then a Yugoslavian company and German television. In 1968, the BBC began broadcasting *The White Horses* dubbed into English as late Monday afternoon viewing at a time when pupils would be arriving home from school. Although only thirteen episodes were ever made, the series was aired – and remained popular – for more than ten years.

The popularity of horses in children's television programmes continues. In the second and third decades of the twenty-first century, on both pay-to-view and Freeview channels, cartoons where the main characters are horses, ponies or even unicorns abound. The 2018 film *Free Rein* – in which a fifteen-year-old girl from Los Angeles spends the summer on an island off the coast of England and bonds with a mysterious horse – was the winner of two Emmy Awards.

## Triggering memories

More for general entertainment rather than being aimed specifically at children (see above) Roy Rogers and his palomino horse Trigger appeared both on television and in films. In a career spanning almost two decades, Trigger (apparently originally named Golden Cloud) starred with Rogers in more than eighty (yes, eighty!) films and many television appearances: 'a remarkable record unmatched by any other motion picture animal' wrote Joel Dortch when appraising the career of both Roy Rogers and Trigger – a horse apparently so athletic and fast that he could 'stop on a dime and give you nine cents change'!

Another horse named Trigger seen on screen belonged to 'Ernie, the Fastest Milkman in the West'. Both Ernie and Trigger appeared in a comic song written and sung by comedian Benny Hill that was first performed on television by him in 1970 before being released as a hugely successful single, which reached number one in the UK Singles Chart a year later – quite possibly due to its innuendo-filled lyrics!

## Pie in the sky

On chat shows, the actor James Stewart used to tell of the horse he rode in many of his films. Being a friend of my wife's family, often staying with them at their house near Godalming when he visited England, it was a story he also told to Melinda and her sisters when they were young. The horse was called Pie and was, according to the actor:

> ... amazing. I rode him for twenty-two years. I never was able to buy him because he was owned by a little girl by the name of Stevie Myers, who is the daughter of an old wrangler ... He retired and he gave this horse to her. [Pie] was a sort of a maverick. He hurt a couple of people ... He nearly killed Glenn Ford, ran right into a tree ... But I liked this darned little horse. He was a little bit small, a little quarter horse and Arabian. I got to know him like a friend ... I actually believed that he understood about making pictures. I ran at a full gallop, straight towards the camera, pulled him up and then did a lot of dialogue and he stood absolutely still. He never moved. He knew when the cameras started rolling and when they stopped.

Petrine Day Mitchum, who (with Audrey Pavia) is the author of *Hollywood Hoofbeats: The Fascinating Story of Horses in Movies and Television* (2014) explained the relationship between horse and actor as it was seen by the cameramen, producers and studio bosses:

> James Stewart rode Pie in seventeen westerns. They became so attuned to each other that in one film, *The Far Country*, Stewart had developed such a rapport with him that he was able to get the horse to do something at liberty all by himself when the trainer was not around ... and the horse needed to walk from one end of a street to another with no ropes on him or anything. Stewart just went up to him, whispered in his ear and told him what he needed him to do. And the horse did it. Everyone on the set was absolutely amazed, and Stewart just said, that was Pie. That's what he did.

## 'Summer in February'

The book *Summer in February*, written by Jonathan Smith and published in 1996, was subsequently made into a film of the same name released in 2013. While horses undoubtedly make fairly frequent appearances on screen, the main reason for including it here is because of its relevance to the mentions of artist Sir Alfred Munnings made throughout various sections of this miscellany.

Munnings is one of the main characters in what is essentially a 'love triangle' made up of the artist, his friend Gilbert Evans and Florence Carter-Wood. It's a true story – set among the coves and cliffs of Lamorna in far west Cornwall (where much of the action was also filmed) – enacted in the years immediately leading up to the First World War. Actor Dan Stevens plays the part of Gilbert Evans – and by pure coincidence, he is also the narrator of the original audio version of *War Horse*.

## A book, a film and a play
*War Horse*, the children's book written by Michael Morpurgo, was later adapted into an amazing stage play by Nick Stafford – and was brought to the screen by producer and director Steven Spielberg in 2011. So famous is it in all its genres that it needs little or no introduction here, except to say that the film version, scripted by Lee Hall and Richard Curtis, is, as described by the *Guardian* critic and film reviewer Philip French: '… a superficially realistic affair, a cross between the equine picaresque *Black Beauty* and *All Quiet on the Western Front*.'

## A dual role
Cass Ole was one of four equine actors used in the 1979 film (adapted from Walter Farley's children's book of the same name) *The Black Stallion*. Although four horses actually had parts in the filming, Cass Ole was the one used most often – the others being brought in when putting him in certain scenes would have contravened an agreement made between the film-makers and his owners which stipulated he was not to be involved in any situations where he would be required to race, swim or be involved in any fight sequences. His owners had good reason to be cautious as prior to his acting debut, Cass Ole had, over a show career period spanning seven seasons, won fifty championships and more than twenty reserve championships – one of which was Reserve National Champion Arabian Ladies Side Saddle in 1976.

## A national and international favourite
Along with many other famous film actors, Richard Gere is a horse owner. His first one was an Appaloosa named Drukpa and, during an interview, Gere once remarked that 'first horses are like your first girlfriend. You never forget.'

Back in 1944, Elizabeth Taylor starred in *National Velvet* and, in 1978, Tatum O'Neal was the heroine of the sequel, *International Velvet*. In both, however, the four-legged stars far outshone the human ones. In the former, a seven-year-old thoroughbred gelding named King Charles played the part of Elizabeth Taylor's mount, 'The Pie' while in the latter, 'Arizona Pie' was, in real life, a 17hh thoroughbred called Cornishman V who had previously represented Britain in both the 1968 and 1972 Olympics.

Not all that long before she died in 2011, Elizabeth Taylor recalled her relationship between herself and the horse King Charles:

> He was given to me on the last day of shooting and it is a memory that I cherish. There never was a sweeter, more noble animal, and caring for him was a great source of responsibility and happiness. We trusted each other. We loved each other. He lived at stables in Pacific Palisades, California, and I rode and visited him whenever I could. Every little girl deserves the kind of miracle experience that I enjoyed while doing *National Velvet* and bonding with that magnificent soul. My heart still swells whenever I think of him, and I still do – often.

## Hightower – not for sale

Another actress who fell in love with a horse she was given to use in a film – and subsequently wanted to purchase – was Julia Roberts. Julia rode Hightower (who had also appeared in an adaptation of *Black Beauty* and in *The Horse Whisperer*) in the opening scenes of *Runaway Bride* and, towards the end of filming, the director decided to add some extra screen footage – some of which required the presence of Hightower. Unfortunately, the horse was already at work on another film in Los Angeles so the studio arranged for Hightower to be brought back to the set location in order that

Ms Roberts could ride him for the closing scenes. Having thus formed an affinity with her mount, the actress then attempted to buy him – but was told (quite firmly) that he was 'not for sale'.

Viggo Mortensen, perhaps best known for his roles as Aragorn in *Lord of the Rings* and for his part in *Hidalgo* (a film in which much of the action involves a man's relationship with his horse) was more successful than Julia Roberts and, once filming had finished, ended up buying his equine co-actors – and Mortensen even rode one of them (by the name of T.J.) onto the red carpet at the premiere of *Hidalgo*!

## Taking the biscuit

'A homeless jockey, a millionaire, a washed-up cowboy and a horse named Seabiscuit are the four unlikely heroes who found hope in each other and inspired an entire generation' – so runs the subtext of the 2003 film *Seabiscuit* based on Laura Hillenbrand's 1999 book, *Seabiscuit: An American Legend*. In May 1947, on the death of Seabiscuit (of a heart attack at the age of fourteen), Pulitzer Prize-winning sportswriter Walter Wellesley 'Red' Smith wrote in the *New York Herald Tribune*:

> ... let's talk about the death of Seabiscuit the other night. It isn't mawkish to say there was a racehorse, a horse that gave race fans as much pleasure as any that ever lived, and one that will be remembered as long and as warmly. If someone asked you to list horses which had, apart from speed or endurance, some quality that fixed the imagination and captured the regard of more people than ever saw them run, you've had to mention ... Seabiscuit ... It wasn't primarily his rags-to-riches history which won [him] his following, although reaching success from humble beginnings never dims a public figure's popularity. It wasn't the fact that he won more money than any other horse up to his time, although that

hurt neither his reputation nor his owner. He wasn't a particularly handsome horse, nor especially big or graceful, and he was never altogether sound ...

With such seemingly damning credentials (Seabiscuit has been described as having 'a less-than-perfect body with short legs and an initially lazy personality') it was as a result of his trainer Tom Smith and jockey Red Pollard that the horse finally found his stride and went on to win some big races in America in the most unlikely circumstances – and in doing so, endeared himself not only to sportswriter Walter Wellesley Smith but also to a great many Americans, whether or not they were racegoers.

## Champion of champions

True-life stories and films featured here are not all about the horse; sometimes, as is the case with *Champion*, the on-screen account of steeplechase jockey Bob Champion and his ride Aldaniti, both share equal billing.

In the late 1970s, while at the height of his racing career, Bob Champion was diagnosed with cancer and the film (in which actor John Hurt plays the jockey) charts his journey back to health via multiple courses of often painful treatment and chemotherapy. As Champion's treatment ensued, the racehorse Aldaniti was, by coincidence, recovering from an injury so serious that it was thought by his owner, trainer and veterinary experts that he would never run again. However, as is the way with many stories told of true lives, the facts and circumstances surrounding the eventual well-being of both jockey and horse are far more incredible than fiction – especially when one considers that together, the pair went on to win the 1981 Grand National, much to the delight of both the race-day crowds present and the general public.

## A dream of a horse

*Dream Horse* was, appropriately enough given its content, filmed in Blaenavon in May 2019 and was released in June the following year. It's a true account of a horse named Dream Alliance which, trained by Philip Hobbs as a three-year-old, won the Welsh Grand National at Chepstow in 2009 by three-quarters of a length – and in doing so, won its owners a prize of £57,000. Dream Alliance went on to compete in a further thirty races and, according to the *Racing Post*, won for his owners (a twenty-two-person syndicate known as the Alliance Partnership) a total of £138,646 in prize money.

It might not have been much of a story – and almost certainly not film-worthy – were it not for the fact that the career of Dream Alliance had very humble beginnings, being the foal of a barbed-wire scarred, bad-tempered ex-racehorse named Rewball bought by Jan and Brian Vokes for £350. The stud fees were more expensive (the mare was put to American racehorse Bien Bien; a liaison that cost £3,000) – the money for which (plus the horse's upkeep, eventual training and surgery from a torn tendon in preparing for the 2008 Grand National at Aintree), came from members of the Alliance Partnership, each of whom paid £10 a week into a kitty. Jan Vokes also worked part-time at a supermarket to help with funds and Dream Alliance's early days were spent on a disused allotment alongside an old Welsh slagheap. Of such things dreams – and an extremely successful film – are made!

## Hercules – the rag-and-bone men's horse

BBC Television's *Steptoe and Son*, first shown in the early 1960s, centred around the lives of a father-and-son team of rag-and-bone men, with the son Harold (played by actor Harry H. Corbett) begrudgingly doing most of the work while his father Albert (Wilfrid Brambell) complained constantly about him and life in general. The writers, Ray Galton and Alan Simpson were apparently inspired to create the characters after overhearing some scrap dealers talking in a Shepherd's Bush café.

Harold's rag-and-bone collections were done by horse-drawn cart pulled by their horse Hercules. In one episode 'A Death in The Family', Hercules dies and Albert takes to his bed – and Harold buys another horse which he names Samson. This too appears to fall ill but when Albert gets up to tend to the horse, he finds out that the illness is actually a pregnancy and Samson is a mare. Rather than call her Delilah, which would be the logical name-change, the mare is called Hercules II. Thankfully (we all like a happy ending!), the horse chosen to play the original Hercules remained alive and well for many years with its real owner, Arthur Arnold.

## Out of Town

Simon Baddeley is the stepson of Jack Hargreaves of *Out of Town* fame. As a youngster, Simon would often drive a pony called Pewter and, during the course of the many series of *Out of Town* (which ran from 1960 to 1981 informing, in a very genteel way, its viewers of the countryside, rural life and traditions), Jack could quite often be seen alongside many and varied ponies. Asked whether he thought there was ever a particular favourite, Simon commented that 'Far too many horses passed through Jack's hands, not to mention mine and my sister's while we were at home. All were loved and respected and taught him [Jack Hargreaves] and us different things. Some were a delight at gymkhanas, and in my sister's case, at showjumping. Others served for hunting and hacking and pulling a variety of carts and of course Ghost featured in the latter years of Jack's life as a pack pony as well as in the trap.'

Despite the last series having aired in 1981, *Out of Town* remains popular on YouTube and on DVDs – and the programmes have become a much-loved nostalgic record of life in Britain during a bygone age.

# 10

# STABLES AND STABLING – THE GRAND AND NOT SO GRAND

Stables vary greatly in shape and size – and in degrees of importance. They are essential to the Christian story regarding the birth of Jesus. He seemingly arrived on this earth in a stable due to the fact that 'there was no room at the inn'. However, it appears that, in the New Testament, there is no mention at all of a stable; only that 'he was laid in a manger' – the natural assumption being that, as a manger is part of a stable that is where the birth took place. Nowadays, historians and researchers are inclined more to the view that the typical nativity scene featuring Jesus and his parents with various visitors frequenting a barn-like stable, is an erroneous one. Be that as it may, there is a lot of historical significance to stables. While Jesus Christ may or may not have been born in one, they have, over the years, ranged from a simple shack keeping off the worst of the weather to being extremely grand buildings kitted out most magnificently.

## 'The House at Pooh Corner'

Perhaps the worst of all stables was the one where Eeyore, the morose donkey belonging to Christopher Robin, friend of Winnie-the-Pooh and the animals in the Hundred Acre Wood lived. Situated in an area noted as 'Eeyore's Gloomy Place: Rather Boggy and Sad', Pooh and Piglet built the House at Pooh Corner after accidentally mistaking the original shack which Eeyore had constructed for himself as being simply a pile of untidily strewn sticks.

## Marbled halls

Pooh and Piglet obviously loved Eeyore sufficiently enough to ensure his comfort – the Roman Emperor Caligula loved his horse Incitatus so much that he gave him a marble stable with an ivory stall. In Britain, according to historian, author and broadcaster Lucinda Lambton, writing in her book *Palaces for Pigs*: 'By the late 16th century stables became important buildings in their own right to provide suitably splendid settings for the ever more highly prized horse. Essential for so many aspects of everyday life, horses also developed the reputation of being an ennobling adjunct of their owner ... Externally at least, the architecture of their stables was often as handsome as the houses they were built to serve.'

## Grand designs

Large country residences such as Audley End, Essex; Peover Hall, Cheshire; Berkeley Castle, Gloucestershire; Seaton Delaval, Northumberland and Wentworth Woodhouse, Yorkshire, boasted stable architecture the likes of which can hardly be imagined ... and all for the sake of appearance. In fact, at the latter, the large Palladian-style building designed by architect John Carr for the 2nd Marquess of Rockingham has, it is often said, been mistaken for the main house due to its grandiose frontage. Having taken sixteen years to build, when completed in 1782, there was apparently capacity for 'eighty-four hunting, riding and carriage horses'.

Built just over two decades before the stables at Wentworth Woodhouse, those at Petworth House in West Sussex provided almost as equally a grand home for the racehorses, carriage horses and hunters belonging to the 2nd Earl of Egremont – with living quarters to accommodate thirteen grooms, a coachman and a kennel groom affiliated to the private pack of hounds also kept on the estate. At Florence Court in Northern Ireland, the stable yard behind the main house originally included 'three coach houses, a coachman's quarters, tack rooms, grain lofts' and five 'stable rooms' while at Belton House, Grantham, Lincolnshire, the stable complex there (built in 1685) is important for the number of original features still intact. Recognised as being of 'exceptional significance for its aesthetic and historical value', it is one of only twenty-one Grade I listed stables in England.

## The stable is where it's at!

'Go anywhere in England where there are natural, wholesome, contented, and really nice English people; and what do you always find? That the stables are the real centre of the household.'
George Bernard Shaw

## Stable statistic

- The world's oldest stables were discovered in 1999 in the ancient city of Qantir-Piramesse in Egypt. It seems that they were established by Ramses II (1304–1237 BC) and could house up to 480 horses at any one time.
- In the Bible (1 Kings 4:26) it says, '[King] Solomon had 40,000 stalls of horses for his chariots and 12,000 horsemen' but elsewhere (2 Chronicles 9:25) the same stables were said to have had '4,000' stalls. According to scholars and historians, the latter figure seems the more likely.

- In 1815, when the tenancy of the George inn at Stamford, Lincolnshire, was advertised for sale, it had ten sitting rooms, thirty-eight bedrooms – and stabling for eighty-six horses.
- Nationalisation in 1947 led to much-needed improvements in the underground stables used to house ponies working in the coal pits of Wales and England. Stable walls were whitewashed and electric lighting was installed. Disinfectant footbaths or walk-in troughs were positioned nearby so that ponies could be washed after a shift.
- In the 1970s, the Hong Kong Jockey Club built a set of high-rise air-conditioned loose boxes thought to have been the first purpose-built multi-storey stables. Also included in the complex was a rooftop exercise arena.

## No luxuries, no extravagances

In 1902, *Notes for Hunting-Men* written by Captain Cortlandt Gordon Mackenzie of the Royal Artillery was published posthumously – the author having 'succumbed to enteric fever at De Aar, in Cape Colony, on 24 January 1900'. In the chapter simply entitled 'The Stables', 'Corty', as he was affectionately known to his family, friends and fellow officers, began by saying:

> In describing the hunting stable, I am going in for no luxuries, but propose to detail the essentials for keeping hunters in perfect health and condition without any unnecessary extravagance.
> The necessary conditions for all stables are:
> Good drainage,
> Proper ventilation,
> Dryness,
> Light ... and with these are connected warmth and space.

I strongly advise you not to have anything to do with underground drains. They are very apt to get out of order, and require more care than you can get most grooms to bestow on the matter. If, however, you should find yourself ... occupying a stable fitted with them, be most careful to see that they are thoroughly flushed daily, some disinfecting powder sprinkled down them, and the traps removed and cleaned.

## Living in the loft

Following on from the above, Captain Mackenzie goes on to opine that 'Above the stables I would have nothing. Rooms or a corn loft overhead are impediments to ventilation.' In that, he was most certainly forward-thinking; however, the fact remains that, in many instances, the space above the stables was used, not only for the storage of hay and other foodstuffs (which could often be dropped directly from above into mangers via strategically placed trapdoors), but also provided living accommodation for grooms and coachmen. Most usually, such living space was intended for single men – married coachmen and head grooms being given a 'grace-and-favour', 'tied cottage' near to the stable complex. As to how basic (or opulent) any of this accommodation might have been, the National Trust's 'Stable Project' (begun in 2016) at Belton House, Lincolnshire, discovered 'Original fixtures such as fireplaces and seventeenth-century casement windows ... [and] decorative materials applied to the walls and other surfaces of the ground-floor stables and first-floor accommodation. The multiple layers of colourful floral and flocked wallpaper peeled from the first-floor rooms suggest the accommodation was surprisingly homely.'

## Poor ventilation and bad odours

Captain Mackenzie (mentioned above) was very much of the opinion that any rooms above the actual stables which might have been used for either living space or storage for feed and hay would be detrimental to the well-being of the horses owing to the very real possibility that it was quite likely to impede vital ventilation. In that, he was very different to his horse-owning predecessors of the eighteenth century whose belief it was that haylofts would help keep the stables (and horses) warm. Gradually, however, it was realised that, apart from the obvious increased risk of a fire taking hold (an incident of which is described quite vividly in Anna Sewell's book *Black Beauty*), tightly stacked straw and hay did indeed have a negative effect on essential air circulation. In addition, as Charles Waistell outlined in *Designs for Agricultural Buildings* (1827), hay stored in lofts over stables 'became contaminated with effluvia from stale and dung' and was, as a result, unpalatable to the horses.

## 'The Fire'

At the beginning of Chapter Sixteen in *Black Beauty: The Autobiography of a Horse*, Anna Sewell's eponymous hero gave an account of a fire starting accidentally in the hayloft above his stable:

> Later on in the evening a traveller's horse was brought in by the second ostler, and while he was cleaning him a young man with a pipe in his mouth lounged into the stable to gossip.
>
> 'I say, Towler,' said the ostler, 'just run up the ladder into the loft and put some hay down into this horse's rack, will you? Only lay down your pipe.'
>
> 'All right,' said the other, and went up through the trapdoor; and I heard him step across the floor overhead and put down the hay …
>
> I cannot say how long I had slept, nor what time in the night it was, but I woke up very uncomfortable, though I hardly knew why. I got up; the air seemed all thick and choking. I heard Ginger

## Stables and Stabling – The Grand and Not so Grand

coughing and one of the other horses seemed very restless; it was quite dark, and I could see nothing, but the stable seemed full of smoke, and I hardly knew how to breathe.

The trapdoor had been left open, and I thought that was the place it came through. I listened, and heard a soft rushing sort of noise and a low crackling and snapping ... there was something in the sound so strange that it made me tremble all over. The other horses were all awake; some were pulling at their halters, others stamping.

At last I heard steps outside, and the ostler who had put up the traveller's horse burst into the stable with a lantern, and began to untie the horses, and try to lead them out ... The first horse would not go with him; he tried the second and third, and they too would not stir ...

No doubt we were very foolish, but danger seemed to be all round ... the rushing sound overhead grew louder ... Then I heard a cry of 'Fire!' outside, and the old ostler quietly and quickly came in; he got one horse out, and went to another, but the flames were playing round the trapdoor, and the roaring overhead was dreadful.

## Fast and loose

For generations, horses were tethered in stalls – as in the way of cattle being milked. The system gave little if any freedom of movement – a situation which, at the turn of the last century, Captain Mackenzie abhorred: 'To tie a [horse] up in a stall is false economy, and cruel. He cannot rest comfortably, undue strain is thrown on the back tendons, through the horse being compelled to stand (as he is in nearly all stalls) on a slope, and the animal, when tired ... cannot restore his circulation by gentle exercise, as he does moving about a loosebox.'

In his 1955 book, *A Horseman Through Six Reigns: The Reminiscences of a Royal Riding Master*, Horace Smith pointed out more of the drawbacks concerning keeping horses in stalls rather than looseboxes:

> ... some horses contracted the habit of trying to kick their next-door neighbour, although every night huge chaff bags were hung around the stall posts, packed tightly with straw, in order to try and prevent accidents. Despite this precautionary measure ... I still sometimes saw broken legs when I came down in the morning... Kicking horses are quite dangerous enough in a stable, but I think the horse that breaks loose at night is far worse, for in a large stable he can cause a virtual stampede. I have seen a loose horse which had entered another horse's stall and bitten him so viciously that by the time the nightwatchman... arrived on the scene, the victim's neck was one large mass of raw flesh.

## A Herculean task

Horse owners have long thought that cleaning out stables can, on occasion, be a Herculean task – and while many situations in life could sometimes be thought of as being 'Herculean', the expression almost certainly originates as a result of Greek mythology and the story of the *Twelve Labours of Hercules*.

The stables of Augeas, the king of Elis, were home to many horses (and even more head of cattle) and when, on the orders of Eurystheus, Hercules had to clean them out in a single day, he quite understandably thought it an impossible demand. However, a little lateral thinking resulted in Hercules first making holes in the opposite sides of the building before then digging a wide trench to two rivers situated conveniently nearby. From there the diverted rivers flowed in through one aperture and out through the other and, in doing so, flushed out all the straw, muck and debris, leaving the stable floors pristine. It's a scenario that might seem quite appealing to some modern-day horse owners faced with constant journeys to the muck heap with a wheelbarrow!

## Look at the dust on this!

Thomas Jefferson, third president of America, was an enthusiastic and dedicated horse rider and, presidential duties notwithstanding, would always try to ride for two to three hours each day (nice work if you can get it!). Apparently, a stickler for cleanliness, his stables had to be kept in pristine condition – as had his horses. It's said that, upon one being brought out for him to ride, he would wipe a (white) clean handkerchief along its flanks and if the cloth showed any signs of dust or dirt, Jefferson would send it back to the stables in order that it could be more carefully groomed and prepared.

## Hobson's choice

Given the name of the author of this particular book, it would be very remiss not to make mention of the origin of the expression 'Hobson's choice', particularly as it has a very direct association with this chapter on stables and stabling. There are many explanations around but this one – as it appears in Albert Jack's book *Red Herrings and White Elephants* (Metro Publishing Ltd, 2007) seems the most succinct:

> In the early 1600s Thomas Hobson owned a well-known livery stable in Cambridge. Hobson insisted on hiring out his horses on a strict rotational basis to ensure each animal was evenly worked and nobody was allowed to select a favourite as was common practice in other liveries at the time. The author and poet John Milton seems to be responsible for the phrase passing into wider English use as he mentions Hobson in two of his epitaphs. Milton was at Cambridge University around 1630 so it is quite possible that he was one of Hobson's customers.

## A hay in a manger
As well as being very clever when it came to huge engineering projects (think Brunel and his impressive bridges that have stood the test of time), Victorians were good designers when it came to much smaller things – like a manger for horses, for instance.

Metal (usually iron) hay racks with perpendicular bars – and often with a manger incorporated beneath – were far more hygienic than wooden ones as there was less chance that mites and harmful parasites could linger in the tiny crevices of any that were made of wood. Cleanliness being next to godliness, they could be scrubbed and cleaned more easily.

In addition to the choice of material used, Victorian stable fitters knew the importance of siting hay racks at just the correct height on the wall: if the former were positioned too high, hay seeds and dust were liable to fall into the horses' eyes and ears and cause irritation. As for the feed mangers, they were most often situated at a height which best suited the horses' angle of neck and head position and in doing so, aided their digestion. It is thinking that has not changed much in the intervening years; after all, as the old adage has it, 'if it ain't broke, don't fix it!'

## Keeping in with the neighbours
DIY livery yards have their own particular problems – and stable politics often rears its ugly head. So many opine that their yard is too busy and that all the activity frightens their horse, or that it doesn't like the hosepipe, flapping sheet of tarpaulin covering the hay store, other people's cars, their dogs, the stable tractor and muck trailer, an errant supermarket bag and goodness knows what else. While we all know that, on occasion, a 'bomb-proof' horse will occasionally spook at something it has seen a thousand times before, the onus is perhaps, on the owner to ensure that their animal is trained and educated in everyday life as

is practicably possible. That aside, a few stable 'rules' as suggested below – particularly appropriate if sharing a yard or keeping your horse at DIY livery – might help negate potential conflict:

- If you open it, close it.
- If you borrow it, return it.
- If you turn it on, turn it off.
- If you leave a mess, clean it up.

# 11

# TURF TALK

Horse racing is said by many to be 'the sport of kings' – it's certainly true that it has had the avid and active support of royalty throughout many generations. As Alfred Cope, writing in 1953 commented: 'These monarchs were men and women who loved a good, game horse, loved the thrill in the blood which mounts with the drumming hoof-beats. They loved a race – yes, and some of them loved to ride races too.'

## Royal racing colours

In races with a large number of horses in the field, often the only way to identify them is through the colours ('silks') worn by their jockeys. The colours are owned by the owners of the horses they happen to be riding. It's a practice that was first regulated by the UK Jockey Club in the eighteenth century when, in 1762 that august organisation (founded at Newmarket a decade or so before) stipulated that riders competing in any official race must wear the colours of their patrons 'for the greater convenience of distinguishing the horses in running, and also for the prevention of disputes'. As to the royal racing colours, those registered to King Charles III are the same as those used by his mother, her father and great-grandfather and are a purple and scarlet jacket with gold braiding, with black cap.

## Horses for courses

In the seventeenth century, Oliver Cromwell (as Lord Protector), prohibited racing, mainly, it seems, because of those who frequented the racetrack rather than as any protest against the ethics of racing or betting. Quite simply, race meetings attracted the wrong sort of people, all seemingly intent on nefarious activity: '... how great a concourse of People do usually frequent such meetings and the evil Use thereof by such ill-disposed Persons as watch for opportunities to raise New Troubles ...' However, according to Peter Willett writing his incredibly well-researched tome, *The Thoroughbred* (published by Weidenfeld & Nicolson in 1970), despite Cromwell's efforts, the sport was to become ever-more popular during the ensuing couple of centuries – as an example of which, Willett records that 'In 1762 there were seventy-six racecourses in Great Britain ... and in 1849, a hundred and one courses were in use.' According to the most up-to-date information (at the time of writing) there are fifty-nine racecourses (excluding point-to-point courses) operating in Great Britain.

## Stockbridge – a scene of long departed glories

Throughout Britain there are, if one knows where to look, long-lost racecourses to be found. Sometimes it is left to whoever is sufficiently interested to discover where they might have been through local history websites, or from picking up clues via place names.

In 1953, Alfred Cope waxed lyrical when describing one particular venue tucked away in the hills of Hampshire:

> Stockbridge! The word calls back vivid memories of long departed glories, yet to the present generation of racegoers it seems as remote as the Hanging Gardens of Babylon ...

Today, just outside that little Hampshire village there stands a hill, high above the Salisbury road. If you are able to push your way between the bracken you will, at length, come upon a tiny 'grand-stand', its timbers collapsed, standing amid the tremendous silence which lowers over the great hill of Danebury. All is decay ... and the keen eye can barely trace the oval track ...

Sir John Dugdale Astley, in the second volume of his autobiography, *Fifty Years of My Life* (published in 1894), remarked that, in 1879, he'd had 'a real cheery party at Stockbridge' when the 'Bilbury Club Dinner was held in the Grosvenor Arms Hotel'. The Bilbury Club held their race meetings on the Stockbridge course until 1898 when, because of the combined insistence of the Jockey Club that every racecourse should include a straight mile – and the refusal of a certain Mrs Audrey Barker Mill (who apparently disapproved of gambling) to permit the leasing of her land in order to fit in the extra distance, both the club and its race meetings moved to nearby Salisbury.

## Out of the frying pan and into the fire

In what is now Alexandra Park, London, a racecourse existed from 1868 until 1970. Because of its unusual and quirky shape, it became known locally as the 'Frying Pan' whereby races were run down the straight before horses were then expected to – as described in Wikipedia, 'complete either one or two circuits of the round course before returning up the straight to the finish – round the frying pan and up the handle ...' Racing pundit and television's Channel 4 commentator, John McCririck was a great fan of the Alexandra Park Racecourse and, in an obituary of McCririck published at the time of his death in July 2019, the *Racing Post* quoted his widow Jenny as saying: 'He wants his ashes scattered by what would have been the furlong post at the old Alexandra Palace Racecourse ...'

## Slow and steady wins the race

The record for the slowest time for a winning horse was set in December 1945 by Never Mind II who, during a 2-mile steeplechase, refused the fourth hurdle and was eventually pulled up by his jockey. On returning to the paddock, the rider was informed that all the other competitors had either fallen or been disqualified for one reason or another so he did no more than return to the course and completed the 2-mile stretch at a leisurely pace (in a time of eleven minutes, twenty-eight seconds) – and by doing so, was first (and the only one) past the winning post. History fails to recall the reaction of the crowd!

## Keeping tradition alive

Supposedly the oldest flat race in England, the Kiplingcotes Derby takes place near Market Weighton in Yorkshire on the third Thursday in March as a result of rules drawn up in 1618 which categorically specified the day and month. The rules were created by a forty-nine-man committee who subscribed the sum of £365 – on the proviso that if a year is missed the race must stop forever. So it was that, despite heavy snowdrifts in 1947, Mr Stephenson, a local man, walked and rode his horse along the course. He was the only entry and Harry Ruston, the Clerk of the Course, the only spectator. In 2001, Ken Holmes defied Foot and Mouth restrictions in order to keep the race alive. They obviously breed them tough in Yorkshire as Ken was, by then, seventy-four years of age and was variously referred to as 'Galloping Grandad', 'Mr Kiplingcotes' and even 'Rebel Rider' as a result. Bad weather almost caused the race to be cancelled in 2018, but a single rider completed the course at a safe and sedate pace – and, in doing so, ensured that the rules laid down four centuries before were upheld.

It's an event popular with spectators and costs nothing to watch but don't expect Royal Ascot; there are no grandstands, bookmakers or any of the other fripperies normally associated with a day at the races.

## What's in a name?

No doubt many have wondered how racehorses are given their often-ridiculous names – and by what criteria owners have to adhere to as laid out by the Jockey Club and others when naming a foal. There's often more to it than one thinks. In the UK, all potential names have to first be approved by the British Horseracing Authority and none must be more than eighteen characters in length, including any spacing – which is why one often finds names where separate words run together. In general, names mustn't be potentially offensive (more and more difficult in this easily offended age in which we appear to be living!) or be the repeat of those of recent previous racing greats such as Shergar, Red Rum and others. After a reasonable amount of time, one can, however, possibly get away with naming a racehorse after a past runner.

At a 2024 point-to-point race meeting held at Larkhill, Wiltshire, one of the runners was called Thistimetomorrow – for the sake of any who backed him, it's to be hoped that wasn't when he finished!

## New beginnings

Commemorated by the monument at Farley Mount, Hampshire (see Chapter 5, 'Equine Epitaphs') – and also in a song recorded by the folk group Contraband – the name Beware Chalk Pit has also been given to a more recent racehorse. This particular animal began life as a National Hunt steeplechaser, trained by Jonathan

Geake at East Kennett. His first race was at Newbury in 2008 and between then and 2015 he went to the start-line twenty-four times – winning twice and being placed on ten occasions.

Under the auspices of the national charity Retraining of Racehorses (RoR), Beware Chalk Pit went on to have a very successful second career in the show ring with well-known rider and competitor, Rebecca Court. Replying to a question in an interview for *Horse & Hound*, Rebecca said that he 'has been a superstar from the beginning. He adapted so well to being a show horse and has such a fabulous temperament ...'

The RoR was founded over two decades ago and, in that time, has done much to facilitate and support the retraining and rehoming of former racehorses. The Thoroughbred Rehabilitation Centre has been going even longer. Although in 2016, the charity changed its name and became The British Thoroughbred Retraining Centre (BTRC), it was actually established in 1991 and was Britain's first ever charity 'dedicated to ex-racehorse welfare, retraining, rehoming and protection for life'.

## Champagne and lobsters

Charles Dickens wrote of picnics at Epsom Racecourse on Derby Day: 'Look where I will ... I see Fortnum & Mason [famous London purveyors of high-quality foodstuffs]. All the hampers fly wide open and the green downs burst into a blossom of lobster salad ... mountains of mutton, lobster, tongue, pigeon pie and an incredible quantity of ham sandwiches.'

In 1870, the *Financial Times* described a particular Epsom picnic where, travelling by steam train: 'Major took his own mulligatawny soup, braised beefsteaks, minced pies, cold meats and a pint of champagne for each racegoer ... champagne eases the rigours of the train travel, drunk to while away the tediousness of the journey, oil the wheels of life and improve the temper.'

## Getting too big for his (riding) boots!

Jockey Frankie Dettori is said to have established a brilliant rapport with the late Queen Elizabeth II – and once recalled a conversation between the two of them after a win in the King George VI and Queen Elizabeth Stakes at Ascot: '"That's my fourth King George," I said. The Queen looked at me and raised an eyebrow: "Lester [Piggott] won seven." That was me told ...'

## Level playing field?

Like many sports commentators, John Francombe, a former jockey and trainer before joining television's *Channel 4 Racing*, was not immune to verbal bloopers such as those that *Private Eye* magazine is keen to include in its regular 'Commentatorballs' feature. 'The racecourse,' he one day announced to viewers, 'is as level as a billiard ball'!

## A case of mistaken identity

In 1904, a New Zealand-bred thoroughbred named Moifaa won the Grand National. Although a laudable event, that wasn't the reason why the newspapers made much of the win at the time. Moifaa had (or so they thought), in true Robinson Crusoe fashion, survived being shipwrecked on a desert island and, after subsequently being rescued, gone on to win this most prestigious of races.

In actual fact, it seems that the story belonged to another horse – Kiora – who had also run in the race. It was Kiora who, in January 1901, had been lost from a shipwrecked steamship which had floundered in the Cape of Good Hope. The horse managed to swim to a beach in Cape Town where he was rescued by locals and, at some point later, continued his journey to Britain.

Whether the newspapers had made a genuine mistake in their reporting, or whether the fact that a winning horse that had been shipwrecked made a better headline is open to conjecture. As is often said when talking of certain aspects of journalism, 'why let facts get in the way of a good story?'

## A hero on the racetrack – and in the air

In the 1940s, the Grand National (along with many other things) was postponed due to the Second World War. The last National immediately prior to that was won by a horse named Bogskar – described as 'a spirited seven-year-old' – at odds of 25/1. Obviously the bookies didn't think Bogskar was likely to be much of a threat, but it is the story associated with the horse's jockey that makes the tale even more interesting.

Eric Foley, the jockey originally chosen to ride Bogskar was injured shortly before the race and his place subsequently taken by Mervyn Jones, a sergeant and navigations officer with the Royal Air Force who was told, tongue-in-cheek, to 'navigate the horse around Aintree'. A hero on the day, Jones proved very much a (tragic) hero during the war when, in 1942, on his eleventh flight mission, Mervyn's Spitfire plane was shot down as he headed towards Norway. With no option but to bail out over water, his successful escape via parachute was sadly short-lived and Jones drowned in the fjord over which he was flying.

## We will race them on the beaches

On Michaelmas Day (29 September) the inhabitants of several Hebridean Islands off the coast of Scotland would apparently take their horses and ponies down to the sea and race them along the beaches. According to Quentin Cooper and Paul Sullivan, co-authors of *Maypoles, Martyrs and Mayhem* (Bloomsbury Publishing, 1994): 'The horses were ridden bareback, and the harnesses were made of straw. This was a survival of a sea-god festival.'

## The Midnight steeplechase

On the night of 10 March 1890, eleven jockeys in full hunting gear all lined up to ride a pre-determined course consisting of six fences; each of which had to be jumped twice. Over the top of their hunting clothes they wore either their own nightgowns or, according to reports at the time, those borrowed from others – at least one of which was a 'pink gossamer nightie, beribboned and frilled ...'

Subsequently known as the Melton Midnight Steeplechase, it was not the first such madcap race to be held as, in 1837, two cavalry officers had competed against one another in the moonlight dressed, for reasons probably only known to themselves, in their nightgowns and bedcaps. In 1890, after a particularly good dinner, a group of hunting men hit upon the bright idea of doing something similar in celebration of Lady Augusta Fane's birthday.

Cecil Fane, Lady Fane's nephew, reminiscing almost a decade later, wrote that it was agreed 'a steeplechase by moonlight would be a nice thing for the youth of Melton and the neighbourhood, as an after-dinner occupation, and a change from playing whist or going to sleep in an armchair.'

It was assumed that there would be sufficient moonlight but, as one of the riders subsequently recorded: 'Someone must have made a mistake with the almanac, as instead of a full moon which we'd been told to expect, it was a pitch-dark night.' Undaunted, the organisers prevailed upon the local stationmaster to provide lamps fixed to poles which were placed on either side of the jumps – with a single one being placed at the point at which the jockeys would need to turn for home. Cecil Fane further mentioned:

> The word had been passed around the neighbourhood that there would be sport that night, and the inhabitants of all the country houses and hunting boxes turned up in full strength. Horses were

*Turf Talk*

brought round, boots and nightshirts pulled on and the whole cavalcade started, making a considerable commotion in the generally sleepy streets. Indeed, the Rev. Mr Karney, worthy man, who lived next door to us, was startled out of his beauty sleep, and preached a sermon in church next Sunday, the text of which was, 'Have no fellowship with the unfruitful works of darkness, but rather reprove them'!

Only four out of the original eleven riders managed to negotiate and complete the course – the winner being a certain Algernon Burnaby riding his appropriately named horse, 'Midnight'.

## From point-to-point

Originally, as suggested by the description of the Midnight Steeplechase above, a point-to-point race was one where the starters all congregated at a given place and were told to make the best of their way to another point, ordinarily a high tree, a church steeple (from whence comes the term 'steeplechasing') or a barn on a hill and, having got there, to return as quickly as possible to the starting post.

Nowadays, point-to-points are generally organised and run under rules and regulations designed for the well-being and safety of both jockeys and horses but there is, nonetheless, still one held annually that bears great similarity to the way the original point-to-points were conducted. Every Boxing Day, in Hampshire's New Forest, riders are given the location of a meeting place just a few days (maybe a week) beforehand and, on arrival, an official starter then takes them to a previously undisclosed starting point – some riders having absolutely no idea where they are when the race begins (and probably less so when it ends!). While the jockeys can be anyone (some are local commoners on the Forest), the equine competitors are required to be either pure-bred, or part-bred New Forest ponies.

## A princely pastime

Edward VIII might have been short lived as a king (abdicating the Crown in favour of divorcee Wallis Simpson) but he had a far longer career as an extremely proficient horse rider, particularly when careering across open countryside and over high obstacles as he competed in point-to-points – in which he had mixed fortune. As the Prince of Wales, competing at the Army Point-to-Point at Arborfield Cross, Berkshire, both he and his horse fell in the last race. The prince was kicked in the face and ended up in bed at St James's Palace. The newspapers, seemingly as obsessed with royalty then as they are now, had much to say on the subject – as Peter Holt, writing in *The Keen Foxhunter's Miscellany* (Quiller Publishing, 2010) notes:

> The Press claimed the future monarch was putting himself in too much danger. They said he was a hopeless rider, continually falling off ... Letters appeared in the papers saying Edward should quit. Prime Minister Ramsay MacDonald asked him to tone down his riding. He took no notice and continued to race and hunt furiously. It was only in 1928 when the King fell ill that Edward finally gave up. His mother Queen Mary asked him to stop racing and stick to hunting. But racing had become his first love and hunting was second best. In a fit of pique, he sold his horses and surrendered his digs at Melton [used as a base for hunting]. A few months later he met Wallis Simpson. Perhaps things would have turned out better if he had stuck to horses.

In 1953, Alfred Cope was of similar sentiment when he wrote that 'It would be interesting to know what renown the prince might have achieved had he been left to pursue his riding undisturbed ... With his abdication all conjecture was silenced.'

## 12

# IN PURSUIT OF THE UNEATABLE

One of Oscar Wilde's innumerable famous quotes was: 'The English country gentleman galloping after a fox: the unspeakable in full pursuit of the uneatable' – quite often minimised or paraphrased to 'the unspeakable in pursuit of the uneatable'. It referred to his obvious distaste of those who favoured fox hunting as a rural activity and it is a quote frequently used nowadays by those opposed to any form of hunting with hounds.

The times they are a-changing. Fox hunting was banned as a result of the Hunting Act 2004 and replaced by 'trail hunting' in which an artificial scent is used. That to one side, more and more are preferring other forms of the sport; either following a pack of draghounds or hunting the 'clean boot' – an activity in which bloodhounds follow the scent of human runners or 'quarry'. With such hunting (especially the latter form), it seems that many who would never have hunted a couple of decades ago are now doing so – and both they and their horses are loving the opportunity to ride over parts of the countryside to which they would never usually have access.

Hunting in the past has, however, been enjoyed by many – and has been written about by countless authors, ranging from Anthony Trollope to R. S. Surtees who created the famous character, John Jorrocks – a sporting cockney grocer whose exploits are covered in titles such as *Jorrocks' Jaunts and Jollities*, published in 1838. With all that in mind, it would be a shame not to mention at least a few (often amusing) aspects of the 'sport' – including this quote, taken from Surtees' *Mr Sponge's Sporting Tour* (1853) when, while out hunting, Cupid's arrow seemingly hit the eponymous hero hard:

> ... something shot through Mr Sponge's pull-baker coat, his corduroy waistcoat, his Eureka shirt, Angora vest, and penetrated the very cockles of his heart. He gave her such a series of smacking kisses as startled her horse and astonished a poacher who happened to be hid in the adjoining hedge.

## Which came first?

From an obituary in a 1935 issue of *The Polo Monthly*:

> Young George's first day with hounds was rather inglorious. They met at Hatfield, and the diminutive George distinguished himself on a little pony called Bluebell by pursuing the fox before hounds came out of covert. There was a procession across the park: first the fox, then the small boy, with the hounds a bad third. The hunt in this order did not last long, for the pony stopped dead at a small ditch and shot George into the bottom of it, where he lay while the pack in full cry streamed over him. When rescued he was sent home in ignominy in the carriage with his nurse and the babies, who had come to see the fun.

## On borrowing a hunter

Wise words from *The Habits of Good Society: A Handbook of Etiquette for Ladies and Gentlemen* published circa 1859, author unknown: 'Never accept the loan of a friend's horse, still less an enemy's, unless you can ride very well. A man may forgive you for breaking his daughter's heart, but never for breaking his hunter's neck.'

## It's quicker by rail

In the late 1800s, those who lived in London and yet wanted to ride to hounds might well have chosen to keep their horses in town and take them down to the country by train on hunting mornings. It was even possible to send a horse or hireling onward to be stabled close to the meet ahead of your own arrival. The 8th Duke of Beaufort writing in 1885, told his readers that 'convenient trains serve practically all of the packs within easy reach of London' and went on to give a list of the most useful stations from which to depart and alight. In addition, *Baily's Hunting Directory* regularly printed the whereabouts of stations nearest to where hounds were kennelled or where meets frequently took place.

## Boxing clever

An animal that will happily load and unload into and from either a horsebox or trailer towed behind a vehicle makes life easier for all concerned – and will certainly save time (and frustration), particularly at the end of a day when, in winter, the hours of daylight are short and everyone is eager to get home. Sometimes, however, comparatively little thought is given as to how a horse or pony might react when faced with being loaded in order to get it to the meet or, indeed, any other equestrian event. How alien it must feel going into the unknown the very first time he or she is expected to walk up that ramp.

Much more can be achieved with patience and gentle training than it can by coercive methods and ill-temper. An animal that trusts its handler is far more likely to box than one that doesn't feel comfortable with the person leading so undoubtedly the most important factor is gaining that trust – and then accustom the horse or pony by letting it get used to the transport while at home and in a place it knows. Some owners leave the trailer in the field where the horse grazes, others feed either on the ramp or actually in the trailer in order to show that there really is nothing to fear.

No matter how it's achieved (and rewards often help), it should always be remembered that entering a small, relatively dark enclosed space is not natural to a 'fight or flight' animal and, until he or she is confident – and has learnt that there's frequently something pleasant and enjoyable at journey's end (a day's hunting, a hack in the countryside, a gallop along the beach or even the mental stimulation of a showground) – what we are asking of our animal goes against their natural instincts. As one horse owner said recently: 'We need to be more grateful of what horses are willing to do for us and more understanding of why they say "no" when they do.'

## Hacking 'hacks' to consider

Although many nowadays use a horsebox or trailer when taking their horses and ponies to the meet of hounds, if distance permits, some much prefer to hack there and back. Here are a few things to consider when contemplating doing so during the winter months when, on a bad day weatherwise, darkness might fall by late afternoon.

- Pre-plan as safe a route as possible (using minor roads/bridlepaths etc.) with the aid of an Ordnance Survey map.
- Make sure you have a mobile phone – and that it includes ICE (In Case of Emergency) contact details.
- Have a small head torch and/or cyclists' flashing front and rear lights in one's pocket or saddle bag – modern ones are so small they take up little room.

*In Pursuit of the Uneatable*

- Likewise, carry a high-vis nylon gillet/vest.
- Consider having someone drive behind you when hacking back in the dark.
- Allow yourself plenty of time. For the sake of your horse, remember that a 'hound jog' of 6 miles per hour is a steady pace at which to hack – although one huntsman to whom I spoke mentioned that if hacking without hounds alongside, up to 8 miles per hour is comfortable for a fit horse.
- Attempt to gauge the time you'll need to leave the hunting field in order to arrive back at the yard before dark.

## Do as I say, not as I do

In 1930, Lord Leconfield's patience was obviously being sorely tried by certain members of the hunting field and, as a consequence, felt it necessary to issue an advisory note to the mounted followers of his hounds. It began with: 'Lord Leconfield hopes that in making the following observations he will not give offence or be misunderstood' – and followed with a few salient points before then terminating his somewhat terse printed missive with the words: '... I cannot hold myself responsible for what I may say to those who fail to observe these elementary rules'!

## 'D'ye ken John Peel?'

Commemorated in song, John Peel was a nineteenth-century farmer who lived at Caldbeck to the north of Skiddaw in the Lake District. He had six sons and six daughters and was, out of necessity, hard-working, for as well as paying for his domestic and business expenses, his farm had to bear the cost of his fox-hunting interests – about which he was fanatical.

Peel was, according to *The John Peel Story*, written by W. R. Mitchell in 1968 as part of the *Dalesman* series of paperbacks: 'part rider, part pedestrian when he took to the trails of the foxes'. When he rode, it was on a brown Fell pony cross named Dunny and as Mitchell mentions, the sight 'must have been incongruous, for he was a tall man who rode with a particularly short stirrup; his knees almost up with the saddle'. When, for whatever reason, Peel had cause to dismount, his pony apparently followed him about like a dog and when he found it difficult to remount (as when he had been celebrating at a local inn – apparently a not uncommon scenario) Dunny could, according to Mitchell, 'be relied upon to kneel in order to assist his owner as much as possible'.

## Taking a tumble – and paying for the privilege

For fun, many hunts have what are referred to as the 'Tumbler's Club' – the idea being that anyone who falls from their horse during the day pays a small fine (usually to the funds of the hunt club or similar) and in some instances, those that have fallen off most are gifted a small prize at the end of the season. It seems to be an idea which originated back in the late eighteenth or early nineteenth century when some mounted regiments that followed hounds on their days away from barracks had a rule that any officer who suffered an 'involuntary dismount' was subject to a fine.

## You're having a laugh

Jimmy Edwards, the fabulously moustachioed English comedy writer and actor of the 1950s and 1960s was, despite his size, a great horse rider and keen follower of hounds – and was, in fact, a joint master of the Old Surrey and Burstow Hunt between 1972 and 1974 and again between 1979 and 1981.

During the same era, English character actor and comedian Terry-Thomas shared similar fame and fortune in films and on television – and also hunted with the Old Surrey and Burstow in the 1950s. Terry-Thomas's interest and love of horses is said to have been inspired by his uncle George Hoar who was a horse dealer.

In 1959, while riding in Hyde Park on a very wet day wearing a deerstalker hat and carrying an umbrella, Terry-Thomas was (for some unexplained reason) interviewed by a television reporter from the BBC. Asked about the headwear, the actor replied: 'I've got this hat on because it keeps the sun off the back of your neck … and if I fall off, it keeps the mud out of your ears too.'

Reporter: 'Do you ride well?'

Terry-Thomas: 'I would say I'm an incredibly good rider as sometimes I've been out here for an hour and not fallen off once … I've won some cups … I have my egg out of one of them practically every morning.'

## Jute rugs? No sweat

In today's equestrian world there is a huge variety of horse rugs but, way back when, Jute rugs for the stable and New Zealand rugs for turning a horse out into the field were virtually the only options available to anyone who wished to treat their horse well after a day's hunting.

Damp or sweaty from the exertions and excitements of the day, a hunter was often dried with the aid of some straw and an old-fashioned jute rug. After 'whisping' (some spell it 'wisping') off the worst of the wet and mud with a handful or two of straw, it was common practice to 'thatch' a layer of it over the animal's back and keep it in place under a jute stable rug put on upside-down (with the felt liner uppermost). This in turn was secured by a 'roller' strap belted under the belly. By the time an hour or so had passed, any sweat had wicked its way through the straw and rug, leaving the horse warm and dry. The rug could then be removed and the straw discarded. A stable rug (or the same Jute rug reversed back to its correct side if the owner couldn't afford a selection) would ensure that, after a feed, the animal was tucked up warm and dry for the night. Any extra warmth that might be needed was provided by army surplus blankets bought from the local ex-military store. Laid over the horse with a neat triangle behind the withers, the blanket was then folded back over the rug and secured with the roller.

It is easy to look back at many aspects of the past while wearing the proverbial rose-tinted spectacles and not all that long ago, a post on X (formerly known as Twitter) reminisced about all the above. It was one that elicited several comments and memories. Someone mentioned the 'wonderful smell of straw, damp horse and jute rug [and] the steam that used to come off them ...' Another commented that she still thatched her ponies 'if they are wet and need a rug on' but admitted that she found 'the modern rugs of today a godsend ... Canvas outdoor rugs and Jute rugs were heavy and hard to dry.' She wasn't wrong, particularly when it came to the old-fashioned New Zealand rugs with leather straps which, although they almost never let water permeate, were a considerable weight when wet – and did indeed take ages to dry. Still, as hard to handle as they were, it seems that such rugs and methods are still thought of with affection by some horse and pony owners.

## Sweaty or merely glowing?

The well-known phrase: 'Horses sweat, men perspire and ladies merely glow' is thought by many to have originated from Victorian etiquette guides – but as to the actual source it seems that no one is quite certain.

## 13

# GETTING INTO THE HABIT

Out riding, whether hunting or simply to be seen in fashionable places such as Rotten Row in Hyde Park, London, lady riders were expected to dress appropriately. Advice given to 'young ladies' in 1860, observed the following:

> A lady's dress on horseback cannot be too plain: a well-fitting black or dark blue riding habit made without any trimming, only buttoned down the front, the usual riding hat, and black veil if required. No ornaments or ribbons, on any account, should be worn on horseback. Linen collar and cuffs fastened with small gold stud or brooch, and doeskin, or any nice gloves will complete the dress.

## For safety's sake

Michael Billett writing in *A History of English Country Sports* (Robert Hale Ltd, 1994) mentions that, while out riding during the early to middle part of the Victorian era, ladies wore 'wide double skirts, the hems of which were weighted down with lead weights'. By the end of Victoria's reign – and into Edwardian times, Billett tells us that 'the safety split half-skirt or apron' (designed by a certain Alice Hayes), had come 'into fashion'. The skirt '... was shaped so that it could not catch on the pommel of the side-saddle in the event of a fall and the rider could not be dragged'.

## Shielded from embarrassment

In 1838, an unknown scribe drew up a list containing eight pieces of advice for the lady equestrian. Number five on the list was this:

> The only inducements for a gentleman to ride on the left of a lady, would be, that, by having his right hand toward her, in case of her needing assistance, he might, the more readily and efficiently, be enabled to afford it, than if he were on the opposite side; and, should any disarrangement occur in the skirt of her habit, he might screen it until remedied.

## On mounting for ladies

More from *The Habits of Good Society: A Handbook of Etiquette for Ladies and Gentlemen* (see also, 'On borrowing a hunter' in the previous chapter):

> The lady, having gathered up her skirt, and holding it in her left hand, must place herself as close as possible to the horse, with her face towards the animal's head, and her right hand on the pommel. The gentleman, whose part and privilege it is to assist her, having first obtained her consent to do so, then places himself at the horse's shoulder, with his face towards the lady, and, stooping a little, places his right hand horizontally at a convenient elevation from the ground. On the palm of this hand the damsel sets her sweet little left foot, and it is then the gentleman's duty to lift it with a gentle motion as she springs herself upwards.

## The interesting life of 'Skittles'

Out on the hunting field – and when in London, riding on Hyde Park's Rotten Row – Catherine Walters became known as being something of a fashion icon and many ladies of the day copied her style, particularly when it came to the subject of her beautifully fitted bespoke riding habits. Born in 1839 (she died in 1920), she was almost always referred to by her nickname of 'Skittles'. She was not, however, born into 'society'; her father seemingly worked in Liverpool at employment in or around the docks, and it is said that she had quite a formidable vocabulary arising as a result of listening to dockland terminology in her childhood!

As to exactly how she might have moved from such origins to being out with the 'great and the good' on the hunting field is, although there are several biographies of her, somewhat unclear. One suggestion is that 'her family moved to Tranmere, where her father kept a public house, and the Cheshire Hunt met there, enabling the young Catherine to ride with the hunt.' Another biography puts forward the idea that Skittles might well have worked as a circus bareback rider at some point – a career very far removed from the circles in which she eventually found herself.

## All the gear and no idea

It is not just the ladies who slavishly followed fashion out on the hunting field – as evidenced by this extract taken from *Cross Country With Horse And Hound*, written by American Frank Sherman Peer and published in 1902:

> As no well-regulated family is complete without a black sheep, so no hunt is complete without a swell ... Here he comes now, fresh from his valet ... You feel like betting ten to one the clothes he

wears are not paid for. But no matter. He had to do it. In fact it was the sight of the latest fashion-plate that decided him to take up hunting. His appearance gives a deal of harmless amusement to the other members. He has choked himself with a stock, and wears a corset, or looks as if he did, in his wasp-waisted hunting coat. He wears number seven patent leather boots on a number eight foot. What an unhappy, uncomfortable person he looks!

## If the cap fits

Finally in this section related to clothing on the hunting field, wise words here regarding the modern choice of headgear from an experienced master of bloodhounds who has hunted all his life and occasionally ridden at point-to-points:

I have listened to the debate about the best form of protective hat to wear for riding/hunting – a peaked hat or a skull cap – and there has never, ever been any doubt in my mind. A peaked cap has saved my nose and eyes during face plants more times than I can remember ...

... Now I know what you're going to say – jockeys wear skull caps. Yes, but their form of riding is very different ... Because they ride short, they are nearly always propelled from the horse during a fall; making face plants less likely. In normal riding/hunting, people more frequently go down with the horse, making face plants and injuries from the horse more likely ...

It's your choice, but give it some thought.

# 14

# ONE FOR THE ROAD

An unknown writer, contributing to an anthology published by Daniel O'Connor in 1922, was of the opinion that 'A man who does not love a horse ... is incapable of a genuine emotion. The motor car, the motor lorry, and the steam plough may ultimately oust the horse from the road and the field as a beast of traction ... but in this country at any rate, we do not keep horses only for utilitarian purposes, but chiefly because we love them ... There is something in the spirit of a horse which man cannot resist ...'

## The rise of the 'hackney hell-cart'

The original hackney cabs, available for hire on the streets of London and elsewhere were first used in the 1600s and tended to be heavy coaches rather than the small, light affairs generally associated with London 'cabbies' of Victorian and Edwardian times. By the mid-1700s, it was reckoned that over a thousand taxis of one kind or another were operating in London – a situation that caused much consternation, not to mention several accidents (see also 'Drunk and incapable' below) and led Londoners to refer to them as 'hackney hell-carts'. Things improved considerably when, in the early 1800s, these big, bulky carriages began to be replaced by lightweight, two-wheeled vehicles which had been developed in France. Known as a 'cabriolet', the name remains in common usage to describe a light open-topped motor car – and, in abbreviation, as 'cab' and 'cabbie'. Joseph Hansom, a coach builder in York took the idea of the French design and created the well-known Hansom cab, for which he very shrewdly obtained a patent.

The term 'hackney cab' is still used by some to describe the modern-day motor taxi and one of the goals of The Worshipful Company of Hackney Carriage Drivers is 'the preservation and promotion of what is widely regarded as the most professional, most iconic, and most respected taxi service in the world.'

## High-stepping and fast

Confusingly, given the name, one might expect that the types of horses and ponies known as hackneys, might well have had a direct association with hackney carriages and the taxi drivers of the streets of London. Even though the hackney horse in particular is probably best known as a driving horse and for his high-stepping action, it would appear not. Instead, general opinion seems to have it that the breed has its origins in the horses once found in Yorkshire, Lincolnshire and East Anglia and that the introduction of thoroughbred blood in the mid-eighteenth century eventually led to a type that bred true. The breed's popularity blossomed as the road surfaces of Britain improved and with that, longer distances in shorter times could be traversed. Hackneys were the status symbol road racers of their day and one horse of the era (apparently named Wroot's Pretender) is said to have won a match race of 17 miles by trotting the distance in less than an hour.

## Drunk and incapable

In the nineteenth century when there were many horse-drawn hansom cabs on the streets of London and elsewhere, accidents between two similar vehicles were not unknown, particularly if, as seems frequently to have been the case, one or other of the drivers was, shall we say, a little worse for wear. On Tuesday 25 March 1879, the *Pall Mall Gazette* covered a case at Bow Street Police Court where a driver was charged with being drunk and incapable while in charge of a cab:

> There was no doubt as to his drunkenness or as to his incapability, for the reins were flapping loose in his hands and his lamentable condition was so evident that he was pursued by a crowd of persons shouting 'Stop him!' ... a gentleman, with an agility and a generosity that do him credit, took the task on himself; and, rushing after the cab, he succeeded in getting hold of the horse's head. In the meantime, however, the prisoner, unfortunately for himself, had driven into a hansom cab, knocking over the horse, breaking the harness, and doing damage to the extent of £6 10s. The magistrate, observing truly that it was 'a serious charge', sent the prisoner, without the option of a fine, to gaol for six weeks, and, moreover, ordered him to pay the cost of the damage done to the cab he had smashed.

## Whip, whip, whip hooray!

In the days when most tradespeople used a horse-drawn cart to transport their goods, in places like London's Covent Garden, there were women who acted as 'whip-minders' while the vendors went about their business. They were, according to social historians, 'on duty in the early hours of the morning, from 3 a.m. to 10 a.m.' Why such people should have been required can only be imagined – possibly because the long-handed driving whips were unwieldy to carry around while their owners were conducting business, or even for the simple fact that they were too valuable to leave unattended.

Whip-minding was not, however, the sum total of their task and they saved vehicle space for those greengrocers that paid them and generally looked after their stalls and carts while their owners were out and about around the market. Their intimate knowledge of the market place and where the regular flower and vegetable merchants had their stalls also made it possible for them to offer useful information to anyone in search of a particular tradesperson among the crowded aisles – as well as occasionally to members of the local constabulary in search of the pickpockets and thieves who frequented such places.

## Van about town

Just prior to and during the Second World War, the horse in city life saw something of a resurgence, not least because of the obvious shortage of fuel for motorised transport. Delivery firms found that smaller vans pulled by horse or pony power were, in the way that electric cars are being championed today, actually far better for short-distance journeys about town. As one delivery operator of the time noted, 'with so much stopping and starting, and better ability to manoeuvre' they were a more economic and viable proposition than the petrol-driven alternatives. Sadly, that resurgence was not to last. It's thought that, between the beginning of 1947 and the end of 1948, a great many equines which had up until then been used to facilitate urban trade, were put down due to there being no work for them once motorised vehicles began to be seen on the streets once more.

## Stagecoaches

During the early 1800s a privately owned stage or mail coach which could keep good time and regularly beat its competitors obviously produced more revenue. Although remaining notoriously bad, coach roads gradually improved and, with the invention of tarmacadam, it was no longer necessary for a traveller in hilly areas to use the roads frequented by packhorse drivers who, to avoid bogs, generally chose the upper ground.

In the interests of speed and efficiency, horses were changed every 10 miles or so – and each was generally rested one day in every four. Therefore, the owner of a fast coach might have had in his stables, a number that almost equated to a horse for every mile his particular route covered. The 'Wonder' coach, for example, ran between London and Shrewsbury, a distance of 158 miles and required 150 horses; all of which were the property of a Richard Evans of Wolverhampton. The frequent changing allowed the journey to be covered in fifteen and a half hours non-stop.

The average working life of a horse on such a run was three years. However, doing such a hard job they were at least well kept and fed *ad libitum*. It was thought (according to *The Quarterly Review*: volume 48, published in 1826) that 'good flesh' was no obstacle to speed as horses drew by their weight and not by force of muscle – therefore the heavier the horse, the more powerful in harness.

The really fast coaches, many of which ran between London and the south coast, were objects of such admiration that crowds collected each day to see them depart. There were, of course, many dangers connected with galloping horses in a coach even on level ground. Pairing horses which took even strides was important due to the fact that those which took unequal paces at speed produced a lateral motion which was felt by the coach and its occupants – thus upsetting the equilibrium. When this happened a wheel touching even the smallest of stones was likely to turn the whole thing over on its side. Broken axletrees and the loss of a wheel were the cause of most accidents, some of which proved fatal for both horse and coachman, balanced as he was high on the box.

## Employment opportunities

Eric Delderfield, writing in 1974, mentioned that, during the heyday of coaching: 'The trade gave employment to many hundreds of coachmen, guards, postboys, horsekeepers, horse dealers, blacksmiths, harness makers, wheelwrights and coachbuilders. The inns supplied postboys, ostlers and grooms, as well as their normal kitchen staff, chambermaids, porters, waiters and the like, and the whole business was run with the utmost efficiency and punctuality.'

## Stand and deliver

In the eighteenth century, from the George and Blue Boar inn, Holborn, London, no less than eighty-four stagecoaches left daily for the north, and from the White Horse, Piccadilly, some fifty coaches travelled daily to the west. No wonder then, that throughout much of this period, although highwaymen (and women) operated across the length and breadth of England, they were particularly prevalent along the roads which led into and out of London. It wasn't just stagecoaches that were at risk; so too were the postboys who rode alone collecting and delivering messages, post and (long before the days of bank transfers) cash from various outlaying and remote inns and villages.

Profitable it might have been but a career as highwayman became a less popular option from 1763 onwards when the recently formed Bow Street Runners hit upon the idea of creating the Bow Street Horse Patrols in order to actively combat their nefarious activities. At first paid for by government funding, these forerunners of the Metropolitan Mounted Police unfortunately ran out of money after eighteen months and it wasn't until the early 1800s that a similar task force (consisting of around sixty men, mostly selected from cavalry regiments) was created. In 1829, the Metropolitan Police Act helped establish a more legislated force – which included a mounted section.

# 15

# AT YOUR SERVICE

In areas where crime rates are higher than they should be, it's an oft-repeated opinion that we need a greater police presence on the streets. On the roads of London and other metropolitan areas, police horses and their riders are still a viable – and very visible – deterrent but their duties are not always confined to the criminal element of society. In 2014, trials conducted by researchers from Oxford University noted that 'mounted police units generated around six times more public interest than foot patrols ...' and Dr Ben Bradford, the study's co-author, commented that 'Many people react positively to greater police visibility in their neighbourhood, and we believe this translated into higher levels of trust and confidence in the areas where the mounted patrols took place.'

## Name, rank and number

The mounted sections of various police forces tend to name their horses according to established tradition. During the time of police horse Winston (see 'Equine Epitaphs') the Metropolitan Police gave all their 1944 equine intake, a moniker beginning with the initial 'W'. In more modern days, the Greater Manchester Police have tended to name their horses in honour of characters to be found in the novels of Charles Dickens. Elsewhere in Lancashire, south Yorkshire and areas of Scotland, the names seem most likely to be associated with a place located within their area. The Avon and Somerset Police have, for instance, worked horses called Clifton, Mendip, Quantock and Wellington. For one of their latest additions to the force Avon and Somerset have, however, broken with even that tradition and, in December 2022, named one of their horses Mike – more formally St Michael – not after the brand name of the famous store, but in honour of St Michael's Maternity Hospital in Bristol.

## Disarmed with one look

'A man who was armed with a knife has been arrested in Lewisham by officers and Police Horse Putney after receiving a 999 call from a concerned resident.

'PC Lehane and Police Horse Putney responded and on seeing Putney, the man gave himself up and dropped the weapon on the floor.'

Metropolitan Police Service social media, January 2024

## All the colours of the rainbow

As far as the black and white colours of a traditional 'zebra' road crossing are concerned, the striped design signifying most of them offers a high contrast distinction which leaves the police horses patrolling our city streets unperturbed. Not so the emergence of some which are rainbow coloured and have been installed on the surface of London's highways in support of the lesbian, gay, bisexual and transgender (LGBT) society.

In 2022 when such crossings first began to appear, there were several instances of police horses out on patrol being spooked by such markings. There is, in some quarters, a misconception that horses only see in black and white but, as a police spokesman said at the time: 'They may not see colour the way we do, but they are not "colour blind" ... Therefore, the differing shades and patterns of a colourful crossing could suggest an obstacle in the road, causing a horse to shy from something that we, as humans do not see.'

Admitting that the difficulty was 'something we hadn't expected', those responsible for police horse training began to retrain their mounts in order to ensure that the new road markings could be traversed without incident or potential injury to horse and rider. As the Metropolitan Police spokesman told a reporter from the *Daily Telegraph* in April 2022: 'contrary to some speculation ... we haven't sent our horses on diversity training'.

## Where's the fire?

Horses and the part they played in firefighting are an important aspect of urban history. In his fascinating blog (https://beyondtheflamesandmore.home.blog/2018/11/25/londons-fire-engine-horses), retired fireman and historian Dave Pike mentions that

> Horses had been pulling the fire engines to fires for quite some time prior to the creation of the Metropolitan Fire Brigade (MFB) in 1866. First for London's Insurance fire brigades then followed by the London Fire Engine Establishment. Horses were usually kept stabled at the rear of the station, close by the engine house and brought to the engine to be harnessed when the summons for assistance came ... By the mid-1880s the previous methods of bringing a horse from their stables was abandoned in favour of having the horses kept in 'duty' stalls adjacent to their respective engines with a loose harness already fitted to which the engine could be speedily attached ... five pairs of horses were kept at most

stations, with two always 'on watch' and ready to go. The horses on watch had their collars hooked to the ceiling of the engine room by a rope, to ease the weight on their necks. Additionally, other ropes were attached to their blankets so that when the alarm sounded they could speedily be removed and left hanging in mid-air with the horses ready to trot to the shafts of the engine.

## Saving lives at sea

On 12 January 1899, eighteen (some accounts say twenty) horses, around one hundred local people and a team of lifeboatmen pulled the 10-ton lifeboat *Louisa* 13 miles overland from Lynmouth to Porlock Weir in an effort to rescue the eighteen-man crew of the ship *Forrest Hall*.

Weather conditions meant it was too dangerous to launch the *Louisa* from where she was based – leaving coxswain, Jack Crocombe with no viable alternative but to suggest that she should be, quite literally, dragged up hill and down dale in order to get to a place from where the sailors on board the *Forrest Hall* could be rescued. The journey took some eleven hours – the lifeboat and crew arriving at a point where they could take to the sea at six-thirty in the morning. Thankfully, the rescuers and the would-be rescued all survived but, sadly, four of the team of horses (borrowed from nearby farmers and other sources) did not.

Using horses (often hired when required from local owners) was commonplace in many coastal areas where a lifeboat station existed but, for several reasons (a reluctance to put valuable animals in danger and the advent of tractors and motor-driven lifeboats being just two), this particular form of horsepower was gradually phased out – one of the last occasions where they were put to work being at Wells-next-the-Sea in 1936. As the writer of an article in the December issue of *The Lifeboat Journal* of that year said: 'Thus passes away one of the most familiar and spectacular features of lifeboat work, a feature at one time as familiar as the horses of the old fire brigades ... those who saw the race for the boathouse, and the team of four, six or eight horses taking the boat into the sea, will not easily forget what a fine sight it was.'

## Transport for the sick and injured

The Normans apparently used an arrangement suspended between two horses to help transport the critically sick and injured from the battlefield and ambulance carts have been recorded as being used in the late fifteenth century by the Spanish military during the Siege of Málaga. The Red Cross used horse-drawn ambulances in the Spanish–American War in 1898 and similar methods of transporting the wounded feature in many accounts of First World War conflict.

According to the London Ambulance Service, a full-time service wasn't established in the nation's capital until shortly before the turn of the twentieth century – with the very first petrol driven ambulance appearing in 1904. Prior to that, anything that could be said to resemble an ambulance fleet by modern-day thinking was horse-drawn and, by around 1912, horse-drawn ambulances everywhere were being phased out in favour of motorised transport – until, that is, the outbreak of the First World War when fuel-driven military ambulances were unable to cope with the horrendously treacherous, wet, rutted topography and horses (sometimes in teams as many as six in number if conditions underfoot were particularly bad) were the only practical option.

As well as being used for transportation of wounded military in wartime and patients in peacetime, horse-drawn vehicles were also used to carry injured horses. It seems that, in 1907 Robert Fowler, the then clerk of the course at Lingfield racetrack, patented the design of a horse ambulance – initially intended for use at Lingfield and on other racecourses throughout the country, but which was also used in some towns and cities in order to 'carry injured animals with the greatest possible ease and comfort'. Such ambulances were often equipped with hoops, slings and hoists to help move and transport their equine patients as quickly and painlessly as possible.

## *Media vita in morte sumus*

Whether written in Latin or in English, 'In the midst of life we are in death' is not a phrase that any of us are keen to contemplate but the fact remains that, when we shuffle off this mortal coil, there will be a funeral of some sort. Except on the odd occasion – such as when, in December 2023, according to *The Irish Times*, 'Dublin came to a standstill as Shane MacGowan's [frontman of Anglo-Irish Celtic punk band The Pogues] horse-drawn hearse made its way into the city centre' – the final send-off for most people these days will be via a motor-driven hearse.

Not so in times gone by. It's known that horses were used in the fifteenth century to pull the hearse containing the body of Pope Innocent VIII from Rome to his home town of Genoa and in the Victorian era, the deceased of the well-to-do quite often made their final journey travelling in glass-panelled (intricately etched with images of doves and flowers), velvet-draped horse-drawn hearses.

The horses, which were generally black, were often draped in velvet trappings, in the funeral colours of either black or purple – and usually had feather plumes fitted on their heads.

Horses used at funerals weren't always black: unmarried women and children might well be carried in a hearse pulled by white ones. If black horses were required for a particular occasion and none were available, it was not unheard of for funeral directors to dye black whatever horses they had in their stables.

An article written in 1875 tells of undertakers 'not stinting with paint or black lead'.

Funeral horses had lighter work than many equines which worked generally on the city streets and for that reason, had a longer life expectancy – a fact that was appreciated by some of their owners. 'He's earned his retirement by twenty years of faithful work,' said one in 1909; 'If he were a man instead of a horse, he would have been made a partner long before this.' Not all had such a happy ending though. A piece in *The Strand Magazine* dated 1897 stated: 'Worn-out funeral horses, one is horrified to learn, are shipped ... to Holland and Belgium, where they are eaten.'

## Resurrection

Horse-drawn hearses and other vehicles used in public service before the advent of motor engines are periodically discovered after having long been used for other purposes or simply tucked away in barns, sheds and outbuildings where they have lingered forgotten and uncared for – in some cases, for generations. Fortunately, some of these have since been restored by enthusiastic craftsmen and women, both professional and amateur.

At the Inverary Jail museum in Argyll, apparently one of the most popular exhibits is the two-wheeled horse-drawn Black Maria carriage built in 1891. Used by many police forces, this type of vehicle – specifically manufactured to carry six prisoners in narrow individual cells – was introduced to Britain from America (where the origin of the moniker still causes much discussion and several theories) in the 1820s. Wooden in construction and painted jet-black with the royal coat-of-arms and monogram on the side panels, this particular example was, after years of service with the constabulary, seemingly first used as a garden shed and then, during the Second World War, as a farmyard store and chicken house. Eventually discovered by a local historian – and purchased for the grand sum of £10 – it was restored to the condition in which it can be seen today.

In March 2022, the *Halifax Courier* carried the story of a horse-drawn horse ambulance that was found (with a tree growing through it) by local wheelwright Rodney Greenwood in a Lancashire farmyard 'more than a century after it had been used in action during the First World War'. When he first saw it, Greenwood took it to be the remains of an old bullock cart but, on discovering a maker's plate and patent number, eventually realised its true purpose. The newspaper article mentions the fact that after the First World War, the vehicle had been decommissioned and subsequently used at a racecourse to transport equine casualties. According to Mr Greenwood, 'That was its "second life" … now this [fully restored and kept at the Wagoners' Museum, Sledmore House, Driffield] is its third.'

In the first decades of the 1800s, the *Quicksilver* stagecoach No. 209, regularly travelled between Devonport and London. Recognisable by its red and black livery and gold embossed 'G. R.' (*Georgius Rex*), the coach somehow survived the centuries, becoming the main subject matter featured in several paintings as well as being depicted on the type of Christmas card that traditionally included snowy scenes, old inns, ostlers, well-wrapped travellers – and coach and horses. In 2015 the *Quicksilver* came up for sale and was subsequently restored by Mark Broadbent, president of the Coaching Club of Great Britain and a Steward of the Worshipful Company of Coach Makers and Coach Harness Makers.

# 16

# TRANSPORTS OF DELIGHT

What can Tommy Onslow do?
He can drive a phaeton and two.
Can Tommy Onslow do no more?
Yes, he can drive a phaeton and four!

So went a well-known doggerel at the turn of last century and it serves to illustrate the importance and esteem which many had for those gentlemen coachmen who were skilled in the art of driving. A fast carriage and pair offered excitement to such adrenalin seekers – and also the opportunity to show off their skills. There was further incentive in that, by owning such a team, there was a chance to earn considerable amounts of money through betting on one another's prowess. Given the state of modern-day traffic, it seems inconceivable now that just over a century ago, the centre of London was being used as a racetrack by the young bloods.

In addition to showing off their skills with their own carriage and horses, some of the young men about town managed to cajole the Hansom cab taxi drivers into allowing themselves to be driven from point to point in return for a couple of pounds and a written promise to be responsible for any damage to either horse or cab. A favourite course for such events ran down Piccadilly from Piccadilly Circus, along the bottom of Bond Street and Park Lane before reaching Hyde Park Corner. The first cab past the coffee stall picked up the sweepstake.

## Through the eye of a needle
Bets and boasts have always been a part of dining with friends – especially after the second or third bottle of claret! In the late eighteenth century, the Earl Fitzwilliam, 2nd Marquess of Rockingham assured his dinner guests that he was such a brilliant carriage driver he could 'drive a coach and four horses through the eye of a needle'. Called upon to prove his point (no doubt among raucous laughter and much table-slapping), he had a 14-metre-high sandstone pyramid built on the family estate of Wentworth Woodhouse (see 'Stables and Stabling'). In the centre of the thin-pyramid folly was a Gothic arch. Naming the structure 'The Needle's Eye' before then successfully driving a coach and team through the gap provided, history fails to tell whether his lordship ever collected his winnings.

## The price of fashion – and a good horse
The consternation and disbelief of the professional coachmen can be imagined when lighter thoroughbred horses began to be used in harness. A particular gentleman's favourite appears to have been the Cleveland Bay, said then to be capable of a steady speed of 6 miles an hour. This fashion obviously led to higher prices being paid for good horses and, in 1830, when the average stage horse would cost around £30, it was recorded by the author 'Nimrod' that a certain nobleman gave £700 for a horse to draw his cabriolet – a price which must have equalled a whole lifetime's wages of a groom or ostler.

## A queen's recreation

Princess Alexandra, Queen Consort to King Edward VII, was a very keen horse rider – her mother-in-law Queen Victoria was once heard to complain that she 'rode too much and danced too much' – but she took up carriage driving after an illness resulting from the birth of one of her children. In his book *The Private Life of Queen Alexandra*, published in 1940, author Hans Roger Madol told his readers:

> Horses and ponies took to Queen Alexandra at once and she had an extraordinary power over them ... [she] used to drive a pony named Huffy in a light cart suitable for the country lanes ... Mite and Puffy were [her] tandem bays; Bene, Beau and Belle were driven in pairs in a little French carriage, and there was Merry Antics driven in single harness. All the names of her horses were chosen by the Queen herself; bays or chestnuts were always her favourites and she generally used brown harness mounted with brass ...
>
> When staying at Belvoir Castle with the Duke of Rutland, Queen Alexandra wrote in a 'confessions book' some answers to her tastes and predilections: her favourite hero was Wellington ... Dickens the novelist she preferred ... but as regards recreations, there was only one answer – driving ponies!

## Modern-day options

There are many categories of driving – and many and varied are the people who enjoy participating at whatever level. For some it may simply be the attraction of taking out their pony and trap along quiet country roads and lanes on a bright and sunny Sunday morning while for others, it is the competitive element of carriage driving that appeals. While no one (except possibly your nearest and dearest!) generally cares what you might

Joseph William Parkins (Sheriff of London and Middlesex, 1819–20) apparently drove around Hyde Park in a carriage pulled by a pair of quaggas – a zebra-like equine which, it is said, became extinct in the wild in 1878. In 1821, artist Jacques-Laurent Agasse painted *Male Quagga from Africa, the First Sire* – his model being a live specimen. (This image, in the public domain, is from the original at the Hunterian Museum, the Royal College of Surgeons of England, London)

'Shire and Shetland' from Sidney's *Book of the Horse* (1892 edition).

November 'drift' or round-up of New Forest ponies on Stanpit Marsh, north of Christchurch Harbour. (Sarah Benwell)

All the ponies which wander freely within the New Forest are owned by people who have the Rights of Common of Pasture – and must be branded in order to identify the owner. The mark must be approved by the verderers and be clear and simple in design so that it's easy to tell apart from other brands. (Author's collection)

*Above left*: According to Scottish folklore, the Grey Mare of Ballachulish is said to appear on misty nights – and is seeking retribution for those who have ill-treated their animals. (Painting by Mandy Shepherd – reproduced here by kind permission of the artist)

*Above right*: The Bible says that a donkey was the mode of transport used by Jesus Christ for his journey into Jerusalem on Palm Sunday – and, according to legend, is the reason why many have darker hair in the shape of a cross on their back. (Liz Wright)

Image from 1910 showing 'Clever Hans', an Orlov trotter stallion, who was said to have been able to answer mathematical problems and perform other intellectual tasks posed by his handler, Wilhelm von Osten. (Karl Krall, 1863–1929)

 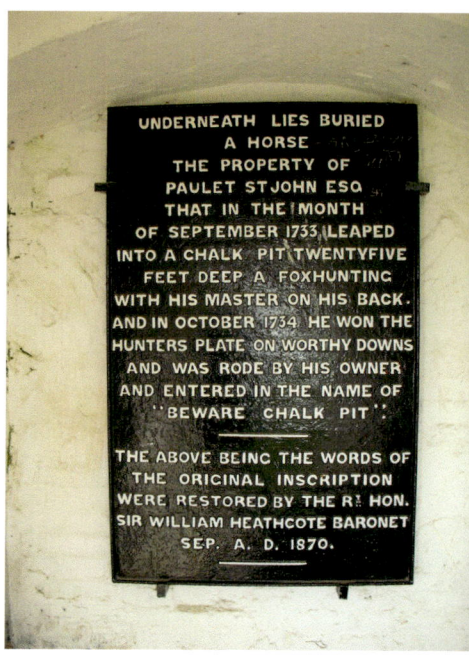

*Above left and above right*: The monument built over the grave of Beware Chalk Pit at Farley Mount, Hampshire – the accompanying plaque gives all the details. (Author's collection)

In February each year, at Central Park, Peterborough; the memorial to Jimmy the donkey (see Chapter 5, 'Equine Epitaphs') is the venue for a small remembrance service held to mark International War Animals' Day. Donkeys and dogs attend; a purple poppy wreath is laid and a minute's silence observed in honour of all animals lost in war. (Liz Wright)

Members of the Household Division rehearse for the King's Birthday Parade (Trooping the Colour) in June 2023. (Sgt Donald C. Todd/Open Government Licence v3.0/ UK MOD © Crown copyright 2023)

Soldiers of the Royal Artillery breaking and training horses, *c*. spring 1915. The location is believed to be on the south coast close to Seaford. The two images are taken from glass plate negatives found in a house clearance. (Alex Warne)

Where less impact is required on the soil, winegrowers in France are increasingly using horses to work amongst the vines. (FreePod/Adobe Stock/Valérie Blanchet-Guillot)

Highland ponies have long been used by many Scottish sporting estates. Occasionally an example of a Highland pony being worked on the hills is referred to as a 'garran', or 'garron', which, in the Scottish Gaelic language, loosely translates as being a generic term for a gelding or any small, sturdy horse of working ability. (Matt Limb OBE)

Sir Alfred Munnings riding on Exmoor, *c.*1943. (© The estate of Sir Alfred Munnings, Dedham, Essex, 2024)

*Above*: Although best known for his paintings of African wildlife and steam engines, a surprising amount of the late David Shepherd's work depicts working horses of a bygone era. *Spring Ploughing* was apparently inspired by A. E. Housman's poem, 'A Shropshire Lad'. (The family of David Shepherd)

*Right*: *Brewers Horse* – a sculpture by Gill Parker – on display at Sculptures by the Lakes, Dorset. (Melinda Hobson)

*Below*: *Cruising* – a life-size sculpture in copper wire of a horse and rider jumping over a hedge – by Rupert Till. (Rupert Till)

The stables at Seaton Delaval Hall, Northumberland. Both in the UK and abroad, royal residences and large country houses often boasted ornate stable architecture and beautiful indoor furnishings. Internally, they were designed for practicality and the health of the horses – but much was also for the sake of appearance. (David Parks)

A lack of land or stabling doesn't necessarily preclude ownership of some kind of equine – as one horse lover living in the picturesque village of Milton Abbas, Dorset, has proved! (Melinda Hobson)

At a point-to-point meeting, the winning jockey and owner pose for photographs while the winning horse is cooled down with cold water. Research has shown that applying cold water over the whole of the horse's body after strenuous exercise helps bring down core body temperature by drawing heat from the muscles. (Author's collection)

Martin and Philippa Whitley own the Recycled Racehorse Falconry Team and work with ex-racehorses to give them a new role in life – an instance of which combines the art of riding and that of falconry. They are asked to give demonstrations all over the country, including Newmarket Racecourse. (Martin and Philippa Whitley)

*Left*: Sartorial advice of the 1860s stated that 'A lady's dress on horseback cannot be too plain: a well-fitting black or dark blue riding habit made without any trimming, only buttoned down the front, the usual riding hat, and black veil if required.' In 1902, American, Frank Sherman Peer said of the man new to hunting that 'His appearance gives a deal of harmless amusement … He has choked himself with a stock, and wears a corset, or looks as if he did, in his wasp-waisted hunting-coat. He wears number seven patent-leather boots on a number eight foot. What an unhappy, uncomfortable person he looks!' (Illustration by Claud Lovat Fraser)

*Below*: Side-saddle elegance – with an appropriately grand backdrop! (Author's collection)

With their high-stepping fast action, Hackneys were once the status symbol road racers of their day but are now infrequently seen other than at some of the major shows. (Melinda Hobson)

A clear polycarbonate visor and nose protector is often used by many mounted police sections to protect their horses in a riot situation. The visor is shaped to fit around the animal's head and eyes and is attached to the bridle by means of hooks and loop-straps. (Mario Beauregard/Adobe Source/Valérie Blanchet-Guillot)

*Left*: In Britain, driving a five-in-hand (three at the front, two at the back) is known as a 'hammerhead' formation. In North America, as a 'pickaxe'. Translated, the Spanish apparently refer to it as 'half-power'. (Alan and Paulette Coe of Layer Marney Horse Drawn Carriages)

*Below*: HRH Prince Philip competing at Baronscourt, Newtonstewart, Northern Ireland, *c.*1997. (Rachel Green)

At the Olympic Games of Ancient Greece, equitation competition centred largely around chariot racing – while the modern-day Olympics fail to include this exciting spectacle, those wishing to experience a taste of what it may have been like, can visit the Puy du Fou theme park in France to watch *Le Signe du Triomphe* spectacular! (Author's collection)

Hours of work go into their preparation but it's all worth it as the immaculately presented turnouts parading in the main ring at summertime agricultural shows are always appreciated by the spectators. (Melinda Hobson)

Ben Atkinson of Atkinson Action Horses, is well known both nationally and internationally for his performances around the shows – and also for his training seminars and equine film work. (Melinda Hobson)

Gymkhana and Pony Club style games are well supported at many country shows and similar events. (Melinda Hobson)

Several years apart (but both on the internationally renowned horse, Bouncer), Judy Crago, one of Britain's most successful top international riders and her son Paul, tackle the infamous Derby Bank at Hickstead in this composite photograph gleaned from the family archives. (Paul Crago)

*Right*: A 'cabriole à la main' being performed at the Cadre Noir, Saumur, France. (Alain Laurioux/CC BY-SA 3.0/CC BY-SA 4.0 International)

*Below*: In a long-term project that began in 1872, Eadweard Muybridge wanted to discover whether there was ever a moment mid-stride where all four hooves were off the ground at once – and, with the aid of several cameras (and a horse named Sallie Gardner owned by Leland Stanford, Muybridge's sponsor), set about proving that there was. (This sequence of photos is in the public domain, but is provided directly by the Library of Congress Prints and Photographs Division.)

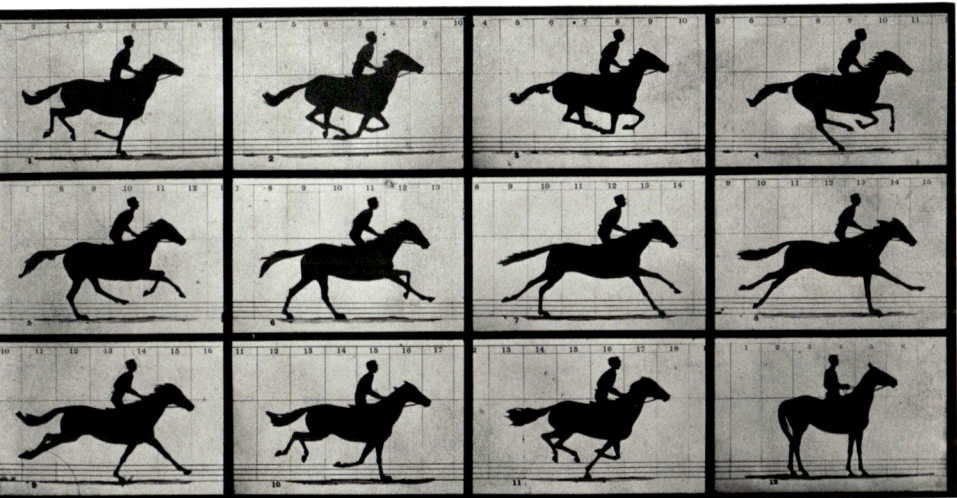

Typically, the balls used in a game of polo played on grass are white: in snow polo, the balls are larger and, for obvious reasons, coloured bright orange/red. (H P/Adobe Stock/Valérie Blanchet-Guillot)

'Tom Pearce, Tom Pearce, lend me your grey mare' is the first line of the well-known Devonshire folk song 'Widecombe Fair', which is thought to have originated in the early 1800s. Widecombe Fair is still held annually and, appropriately enough, is where this particular image was taken. (Author's collection)

'Has he *fashion* enough, think ye, Sir?' An illustration for *The Sport of Our Ancestors* (Lord Willoughby de Broke, 1925) by renowned equine artist G. D. Armour, 1864–1949. (See Chapter 21, 'All the Fun of the Fair' and Chapter 8, 'Equine Artists'.)

wear when out trotting along sequestered tracks and byways with just the jingle of harness, the whirring rhythm of the trap wheels and the sound of rural life all about, competitive private driving classes are another thing entirely. In such circumstances, participants are under the scrutiny of a judge who will assess not only the carriage and horses (or ponies) pulling it, but also the turnout of driver and passenger sitting on the box. Their attire must be immaculate and in some instances, as formal as if going to a society wedding.

For thrills and sometimes spills one can do no better than scurry driving where small lightweight carriages are propelled at speed (and against the clock) around the tightest of corners, around cones with balls balanced on their tops and in between slalom poles. While it might be reasonable to assume that the small ponies are the speediest and most suited to getting around a course with the least mishap, that's not always the case and some of the larger turnouts do surprisingly well.

If you don't fancy the wet weather and open fields, it's possible to participate in driving competitions held in an indoor area but if, on the other hand, the wide, open spaces appeal, you could try the intriguingly named spider driving which, as someone described it, is 'essentially orienteering in a carriage [whereby] you and your carriage have to get from one defined point to another in the fastest possible time'.

## More of a partnership

It's the opinion of many that driving any combination of vehicle and horse or pony requires considerably greater skill than simply riding – as one particular carriage driver recently argued: '... in a partnership between the whip [driver] and their horses ... actual physical control is limited because of the simple fact that the bridle and bit are several feet away from the hands of the driver;

there's no leg aids possible and you are sitting behind rather than on top of the animal ...'

## Safety first

The British Driving Society (BDS) was formed in 1957 with the aim of supporting and encouraging people interested in carriage driving in all its forms.

In any equine discipline, accident prevention is paramount – and the BDS emphasise the following safety points:

- Never take the bridle off while the equine is attached to the carriage.
- An active and competent groom should be in attendance at all times.
- Equine, harness and vehicle must be in sound condition and suitable for the activity and terrain.
- When the equine is in harness and attached to the carriage, control must be maintained at all times either through the driver who will be on the box seat, or by the groom who will either hold the reins or a lead rope attached to the bit or under halter.
- No passenger or groom should be on the carriage until the driver is on the box seat holding the reins.
- Before attending a group event ensure your equine is happy driving in company.
- When driving in company never move off adjacent to a horse being put to, unless the driver is happy for you to do so.

## Colourful characters

As with any sport, the famous names associated with carriage driving are forever changing. Some, however, will because of their outstanding achievements, always be remembered irrespective of in which decades they competed and first became a name in the sport. A few are also what one might possibly best be described as colourful characters!

Someone who worked for the late Alan Bristow on his Baynards Park estate, Cranleigh, Surrey, once remarked in my hearing, 'Some days you would die for him ... on another you could happily kill him!' A man with a fierce temper, Bristow was the founder of one of the world's largest helicopter services companies – and had a fascinating back story. It was one that included winning the Croix de Guerre in 1950 for rescuing wounded French Foreign Legion soldiers in Indochina and, in the 1990s, inventing and creating waterbeds for dairy cows out of thick Dunlop rubber (for which he won the Duke of Edinburgh's Award for Agricultural Innovation). Of greater relevance to this chapter however, during the 1970s and 1980s, Alan became well known for carriage driving (four in hand) and was a member of the British teams competing in countries such as Holland, Germany and Hungary. The team won bronze in the 1984 World Championships in Hungary – other members of the team included George Bowman and HRH the Duke of Edinburgh.

George Bowman is from Cumbria and, appropriately enough, drives a team of Cumberland cobs. Since 1972, George has led the British team to one gold and five bronze medals in the World Driving Championships as well as being British National Champion on nineteen occasions. In addition, he is an Honorary Life President of British Carriagedriving (the UK governing body for the sport of horse driving trials). The apple obviously never falls far from the tree as his sons George Jnr, Barnaby and Robert also nowadays compete. A keen supporter of the annual Lowther Carriage Driving Trials, their father and the late Duke of Edinburgh often found themselves competing against one another. Fortunately it was always good-natured rivalry and, speaking of the duke after his death in 2021, George said (during a media interview): 'We were friends, we would have a drink and a chat and do barbecues ... He was a man's man. He didn't suffer fools and was a plain speaker. I liked that.'

In 1964, HRH the Duke of Edinburgh was elected president of the International Equestrian Federation (IEF) and was instrumental in the drafting of the first International Rules for Carriage Driving. His interest in carriage driving was, quite literally, accidental as it was only when an injured wrist made it difficult for him to continue playing his much-enjoyed sport of polo that he took up driving in 1973. 'I was looking round to see what to do next,' said the duke in 2017 '... and I suddenly thought, well, we've got horses and carriages so why don't I have a go ... So I borrowed four horses from the stables in London, took them to Norfolk and practised ...' Practice obviously made perfect and he competed most successfully at high-level carriage driving both in Britain and abroad until well into his eighth decade.

In *Thirty Years on and Off the Box Seat* (published by J. A. Allen & Co., in 2004), the duke wrote, 'I am getting old, my reactions are getting slower, and my memory is unreliable, but I have never lost the sheer pleasure of driving a team through the British countryside.' It was a pleasure he obviously passed on to his granddaughter Lady Louise Windsor who, like her late grandfather, is a keen and competent carriage driver competing annually at events such as the Royal Windsor Horse Show.

# 17

# SHOW TIME

Not all that long ago, many horse shows were held at local level on village greens and in farmers' fields up and down the country. Riding, in-hand showing, showjumping and gymkhana classes were all commonplace and, in almost every instance, organised by dedicated bands of unpaid individuals who took time out to run such events – which were always well supported by competitors and members of the nearby communities who came along to watch.

Today, the immaculately presented carriages and horses parading in the main ring at any agricultural show or similar event still attract the ringside crowds – as do the smart ponies pulling equally smart tradesmen's turnouts. While enthusiastic applause is evidence of the general public's appreciation of the overall appearance and obvious hard work (hours of polishing leatherwork, paintwork, plaiting and equine training) involved with the overall presentation of any equine ring event, there can be no doubt that, as the heavy horses in the shafts of farm wagons and brewery vehicles, trot on by, chains jingling and harness creaking, the sound of the spectators' clapping is turned up a notch.

## Ring craft

Assuming your horse, pony or donkey has been well prepared beforehand (washed, groomed, suitably trained to stand for in-hand competitions and is used to crowds and the confines of a show ring if ridden classes are your thing), a few pointers might help in securing the coveted red rosette.

- Make sure you've checked the schedule for the timing of a particular class – and keep an ear out for announcements over the public address system.
- On entering the ring, walk around (normally in a clockwise direction) as other competitors come in.
- Walk around with your horse nearest to where the judge is standing – so as not to obscure their view of your animal.
- If at all possible, try to avoid being next to a horse of the same colour as yours – if several similarly coloured animals are together, yours is less likely to stand out and catch the judge's eye.
- Keep walking until a steward tells you to move towards a line in the centre of the ring.
- Always pay attention to the stewards and carry out their instructions.
- Within reason, try and allow some space between you, the other competitors and their horses.
- Stand at the head of your horse rather than the side so as not to obscure the judge's view.
- On summer days, flies might be a problem – a fly spray applied before entering the ring might be sufficient to prevent your horse from becoming bothered by them – and failing to show themselves to their best advantage as a result.

- At all times be courteous to your fellow competitors, stewards and the judges: should you be fortunate enough to win a rosette, make sure you thank the judge properly.
- Remember the old adage (Murphy's Law) that 'anything that can go wrong is quite likely to go wrong' and keep smiling when it does!

## Heads and tails

Some types of horse and pony (most usually of the cob variety) have their manes 'hogged'. The majority though, keep their manes as nature intended but even so, there are occasions (out hunting, in competition to comply with tack and turn-out standards, and in several other equine disciplines) where it might be necessary to plait or braid the mane and tail of your horse or pony. It's a practice which looks smart and elegant but is one which began centuries ago for purely practical purposes. The tradition of plaiting the mane is said to have arisen in part as a way of keeping the hair from getting entangled with a sword or weapons in battle while a plait in the tail of a driving horse helps to prevent it from becoming caught in the chains and harness connecting vehicle and horse. Plaiting a tail also keeps the majority of it out of the worst of the dirt when riding in muddy conditions; out hunting it's often possible to see a horse or pony with a plaited tail which has then been further protected by having a portion of it turned up and taped or temporarily sewn into position.

For practical 'how to' advice on plaiting a horse or pony's mane and/or tail, the methods, tips and useful life 'hacks', one only needs to go to the internet where such advice abounds – and where there are many products available which promise to make the task much easier.

## Perfect plaits

How many plaits should be put into a horse's mane is a subject for debate – and a bone of contention in some quarters. Some say it depends on whether one is showing or hunting. All however agree that they should be odd, not even in number. A 'vox-pop' of horse owners well-known in various equine disciplines resulted in the following observations:

- Thirteen is the Pony Club answer.
- They should number nine, eleven or thirteen depending on the length of the neck and thickness of mane – plus one in the forelock – as an even number would create an optical illusion of the neck in two halves. Size and style of plaits vary according to discipline generally.
- Absolutely it should be an odd number ... and should be on the right irrespective of which side the mane lies naturally. Anywhere from seven to seventeen to suit the horse, but not the ridiculous number of tiny, flat showjumping plaits the USA seems to like so much.
- The horse's conformation would dictate style, though I would reserve very small numbers of very large plaits purely for dressage.
- The sizing and spacing is dependent on size of horse, so numbers will vary ... bigger plaits for dressage and smaller for jumping and showing.
- If you want to elongate a shorter, fatter (usually on a rotund pony) neck, use a few more lower plaits and if you want to try and shorten a long thinner neck, have fewer plaits that are more raised in order to create an illusion.

One person suggested that elastic bands could be used to hold plaits in place when the horse is being used in hunting or racing, with a needle and thread only necessary for showing and dressage – at which comment the traditionalists threw up their hands in horror and said that plaits should *always* be secured by needle and thread!

## No more short cuts

Although tail-docking is no longer legal in Britain and many other parts of Europe, it is still permitted in some North American states. In September 2023, Chantal Da Silva, a breaking news editor for *NBC News Digital*, reported that Anheuser-Busch, Budweiser's parent company, would no longer be docking the tails of their famous Clydesdales, long used in promotional appearances at many major US events and in their on-screen advertising. Chantal's report said that 'Over the past year, the beverage giant has faced mounting backlash over the practice known as "docking," which can involve cutting through a horse's tailbone for cosmetic reasons' and that 'Tailbone amputation for cosmetic reasons is banned in at least ten states and several countries, according to the American Veterinary Medical Association … the American Association of Equine Practitioners has also condemned tailbone amputation for cosmetic reasons.'

In Britain, even if a docked horse had been imported from a country where the practice was legal, you would not be allowed to show it at one of the county shows which takes place during the summer months. It is, however, important not to confuse docking with trimmed tails on the likes of Clydesdales and other draft horses often seen at agricultural shows. Where the tail hair has been trimmed level with the end of the dock no operation has been carried out and so it is perfectly legal and above board.

## Keep it natural

The Welsh Pony and Cob Society's *Judging and Showing Handbook 2023*, states that abiding by the rules of the WPCS is 'a condition of competing at our affiliated shows and should be upheld by all competitors ... they are not open to interpretation and any deviation from them will not be tolerated.'

As far as manes and tails are concerned, section 4.5 ('Show ring production') reminds would-be competitors that 'The overall image has to be in keeping within the natural beauty of the Welsh breeds. Pulled and shortened manes and tails detract from this "native" look as does clipping of body hair. Exhibitors and judges alike should be aware that production of this nature serves to do the Welsh breeds an injustice in the show ring. Any act of production which looks artificial and detracts from the "native" look should be discouraged.'

## Make mine a double

Gymkhana games (presumably intended for adults only) during the 1930s apparently included galloping at full speed towards a table, dismounting, throwing back a gin and tonic, lighting a cigarette and then remounting and careering off to the finishing line ahead of your fellow competitors!

## No camping

It's always important to remember that not everyone in your family and circle of friends is as keen on horses and attending shows as you are. One person suggested to her non-horsey boyfriend that he might like to come along to a two-day event and much to her surprise, he said 'yes'. Pushing her luck, she further suggested to him that they could get a tent and stay overnight in the show's camping area. 'A great idea,' said the boyfriend, 'but make sure you get a really brightly coloured one.' 'Why brightly coloured?' she asked. 'So that I can spot you from my hotel room,' came the reply!

*Show Time*

## A show pony of the right temperament
From 'Ponies for Children' (author unknown); an article in *Country Life* dated 31 March 1934:

> Far and away the most important point in selecting our pony is to find one with the right temperament. Make and shape are as nothing compared with this ...
>
> In the show ring accidents are far too frequent; children are often sent into the ring on ponies which are quite unsuited to them. I have seen a child run away with, another bucked off, another kicked by her own pony, another with one who reared, and so on. If a little girl is bucked off before hundreds of spectators consequently takes a dislike to riding, can we wonder at it? In seeking to steer clear of any risk of nervousness, we cannot pay too careful attention to the choice of a pony with the right temperament, and, having found him, we must see to it that he never gets too fresh.

## Good for the child
'No one can teach riding so well as a horse' opined the author C. S. Lewis in *The Horse and His Boy*. On the subject of showjumping and gymkhanas, in 1947, Lt-Col. W. E. Lyons had this to say:

> Showing a pony in the ring is good for a child because it gives it an incentive to improve its riding and its pony, but beware the Swollen Head! Showjumping for children has the same disadvantage as showing. It has the merit though of teaching children to sit forward over a jump but on the debit side it is apt to develop a rough untidy method of riding. Many good children I have seen this year have started to copy their elders (and not always 'betters') and get

themselves into any position on the pony except where they are intended to be – in the saddle.

## Pony club – a love/hate relationship

Mention pony clubs to those who have been members and you are very likely to receive polar opposite reactions. Some loved it, some hated it – there appears to be no in between.

Love or hate, the fact remains that the Pony Club – founded in 1929 (and now represented in at least twenty-seven countries) as a way of encouraging children to ride – has been enormously successful in helping to produce some of the best equestrians; all of whom would, in their early years, have sported the easily recognisable purple and pale-blue tie.

A certain aptitude might be required – as one past Pony Club member recalls, 'Some instructors tend to be of the no-nonsense sort ... if you fall off your horse, you get back on.' Others think it a club for 'pushy' wealthy parents of a certain ilk. Yet more have fond memories of Pony Club – and in particular, the annual camps – and remember learning many elements of riding and the skills taught there.

## These boots were made for riding

Rather than the long boot more often seen nowadays, jodhpur boots were once a common form of footwear for the rider in the show ring, particularly youngsters. In fact, long boots were frowned upon for children and teenagers aged eighteen and under – and for good reason. In jodhpur boots, it is far easier for the rider's legs to bend around the horse and for them to keep their heels and weight down and toes forward. They also made it easier for riding instructors to see what exactly what a young rider was actually doing with their feet and ankles. Long boots, in the opinion of those self-same instructors, disguised much of this – and were only for when the basics had been mastered.

## Jogging along in jodhpurs

Should anyone wish to know how jodhpurs came to be called thus, the online Cambridge University Press (www.cambridge.org/core/journals/journal-of-british-studies/article/abs/one-british-thing-jodhpurs) offers the following information:

> They derive their name from the princely state of Jodhpur in Rajasthan, which was brought under British control in 1818. Originally designed specifically for horse riding, jodhpurs are tight fitting from the ankle to the knee but flared at the hip to provide comfort and mobility in the saddle.
>
> Jodhpurs, despite their Indian name and provenance, are a quintessentially 'British thing' ... [although] originally associated with elite Indian sportsmen and royalty, [they] have become an iconic staple of British equestrian culture, cavalry uniforms, and fashionable leisurewear.

## Hee-haw, ha-ha!

Treated well, donkeys are generally amenable companions and, for the most part, seem to enjoy being the centre of attention when paraded in the show ring. It's not just donkeys that are amenable either; so too, it seems, are the owners. As one long-time exhibitor pointed out when asked to comment: 'There's a great deal of fun to be had from showing. Lots of agricultural shows have donkey classes where, in addition to the more serious breed classes there are usually classes for pets, best turned-out, veterans, child handler and ridden donkey so that any donkey can have a go.' Another verified the friendly fun aspect of it all: 'Horse people get really cross when their horse misbehaves whereas donkey people just laugh!'

## An excuse for merriment
The late HRH the Duke of Edinburgh was known for his one-liners, quips and comments. One – nowhere near as controversial as some he uttered – was this: 'A horse which stops dead just before a jump and thus propels its rider into a graceful arc provides a splendid excuse for general merriment.'

# 18

# A CLEAR ROUND

Different generations have all had their own heroes, both equine and human. In the 1950s, for example, there was Sir Harry Llewellyn who, riding his horse Foxhunter, won some seventy-eight international competitions and brought home the only British gold medal from the 1952 Olympics. Apparently quite a character, in the time he belonged to Norman Holmes, Foxhunter would, when Norman whistled, jump over the hedges between his field and the yard in order to be fed.

In the 1960s, having begun his showjumping career – aged eight – by competing on a milk pony owned by Bingley farmer Jack Baker at the town's agricultural show in 1947, Harvey Smith went on to great success.

In the seventies, Eddie Macken and Boomerang won the Hickstead Derby four years in succession (although not with a clear round on each occasion). Macken had a lot of female fans during the height of his fame – and some even admired his horse! As a combination the two were pretty hard to beat on the Hickstead course. Someone who was there as a young teenager watching on the occasion of the couple's last win remembers that '... it was magical. He [Macken] only came back on the starting list at the last minute and I asked my dad to put a pound on him to win at the betting booth next to the tunnel. It was a fantastic win which me and my friends celebrated by jumping into the water jump after the event!' Others – who may or may not have witnessed Eddie and Boomerang's numerous wins at first-hand – recall that the horse was ridden in a Hackamore bridle which was, at the time, apparently quite unusual.

During the 1980s, the Whitaker brothers' names began to appear with increasing regularity on the show circuit – and have since created a dynasty with three generations involved in the sport. In the 1990s, Di Lampard began a successful showjumping career that last several years and around the same time, was joined by Robert and Steven Smith (sons of Harvey) and Tim Stockdale among others. In the early twenty-first century, names such as Laura Renwick and Tina Fletcher appeared with great regularity and, in the present day, Tim Stockdale's son Joe is very much at the forefront (interestingly, Joe had a choice of going down the route of playing professional cricket or going on the showjumping circuit – and chose the latter!). Other names of note include Lily Freeman Attwood, Helen Tredwell, Harry Charles, Scott Brash, Matthew Sampson and Ben Maher – all of whom are well known on both the national and international showjumping circuit.

## A Cinderella story

In America, Snowman, a farm horse previously worked by an Amish family, was rescued from a lorry bound for the abattoir by Harry de Leyer who purchased him for the sum of eighty dollars. Within two years the pair had become national showjumping champions and were, as some reports describe them 'the Cinderella story and media darlings of late 1950s and 1960s'.

Snowman is the subject of the book *Eighty Dollar Champion: Snowman, the Horse That Inspired a Nation* by Elizabeth Letts, published by Random House in 2011.

## Bouncing to success

During the 1950s and 1960s, Judy Crago was one of Britain's most successful top international riders. In 1960, she won the championship at the British Showjumping Association's National Championships held at Stanley Park, Blackpool and, in 1962, the prestigious Queen Elizabeth II Cup at the Royal International Horse Show.

Arguably, Judy's most famous horse was Spring Fever, but she also had great success with Bouncer. Paul Crago, Judy's son and himself a showjumper of note, remembers that

> Bouncer was bought from Marian Bowden as a novice in the early [19]70s. His original name was Frimley Bridges – the head office of British Car Auctions who sponsored him. Then the Brevit shoe company took over [as a sponsor] ... 'Brevit Bouncer' was a make of shoe! Mum rode him internationally till 1976 when he was loaned to Rowland [Fernyhough] for the Montreal Olympics (... Mum couldn't ride him at the Olympics as she had professional licence at the time and was therefore ineligible). She had him back for one season before she retired in 1977 and Rowland took over the ride again. I was lucky enough to ride him for a couple of seasons (very badly!) after Rowland sent him back to us ... He ... taught me an awful lot in that time.

Judy (who died in early 2023), always maintained that she was the first rider to go down the famous Derby Bank at Hickstead. Whether she was or not, she was almost certainly the first woman to do so.

## Jumping for joy

Judy Crago's son Paul (see above) has had his own fair share of showjumping success and, asked to explain what his typical thoughts might be in the ring, had this to say, 'Jumping clear in a Grand Prix, my initial feelings would be ones of elation but thoughts quickly turn to the jump-off and working out the quickest and best way for you and your horse. The real joy comes after you've won! Different riders react differently; some are very extrovert while others are more reserved.'

## Get ahead, get a hat

On Facebook and other social media, groups such as the Golden Age of Show Jumping and The Showjumping Hub frequently feature photographs of famous showjumpers and their horses from the 1960s and 1970s. Many are seen riding without hard hats (but not in the show ring) – a fact which many who comment, quite rightly decry.

In the interest of safety and self-preservation one should, of course, always wear a hard hat, no matter whether competing in any equine discipline or simply hacking out in the countryside but some commenting on the photographs, point out that the hard hats worn for showjumping at the time were unlikely to have saved the rider in a fall due to the fact that they had no means of holding them secure. While wearing a hard hat was a requirement in the show ring and the 'rules' wouldn't let a competitor start their round without one, they quite often fell off the rider's head as they went over the jumps and many – such as Canadian rider, Jim Elder – hardly ever finished a course with their hat still in position. As one ex-competitor mentions: 'Back then, we only wore our hats in order to be able to doff them to the judges!'

## Taking it all in your stride

Henrietta Knight knows a thing or two about horses – and how to get them to take jumps in their stride. In the 1970s she was well respected for her eventing skills and for over two

## A Clear Round

decades, trained National Hunt racehorses – and has more than 700 winners to her credit (including Best Mate who won three Cheltenham Gold Cups: 2002, 2003 and 2004). In an interview recorded in 2023, Henrietta recalled how, at one time, she took lessons with Swedish trainer, the late Lars Sederholm:

> He had this thing about staying in your stride ... he used to put four single poles on the ground and he had the riders he was teaching run over these poles ... If they were spaced right [and] if you were just trotting along or running along and you met them right, everything was perfect ... if you went at them too quickly you got completely confused and you got on top of the poles and you made mistakes. Even with the four little poles on the ground, it was really interesting ... it's exactly the same with horses: if you suddenly put them out of their stride when they're in a rhythm, then you get the mistakes.

## The importance of a light hand

During the interview mentioned above, Henrietta Knight also talked of the importance of a rider having 'good hands' and explained: 'When a horse jumps, it likes to stretch its neck a little bit and if jockeys have what are called bad hands they grab hold of the reins too much and stop the horse being able to stretch its neck and use its back ...'

In Chapter Ten of *Black Beauty* ('A Talk in the Orchard'), the eponymous hero has this to say on the subject:

> Oh! If people knew what a comfort to horses a light hand is, and how it keeps a good mouth and a good temper, they surely would not chuck, and drag, and pull at the rein as they often do. Our mouths are so tender that where they have not been spoiled or hardened with bad or ignorant treatment, they feel the slightest

movement of the hand, and we know in an instant what is required of us.

Someone tutored by Harvey Smith claims that, when she was young, he taught her to have light hands on the reins by making her ride with an egg in each hand.

## A kind gesture!

Some folk, disgruntled by one person or another (perhaps a car driver who had cut across them or who had otherwise caused displeasure), might well have told others to whom they were recounting the tale that they had 'given them a Harvey Smith' – a hand gesture totally the opposite way round to the two-fingered 'V for Victory' salute famously raised by Sir Winston Churchill during the Second World War.

Harvey Smith was, of course, a showjumping legend of his time – he won six medals at world and European level but is, perhaps almost as best remembered by some of a certain age for holding up two fingers to the judges after winning his second Hickstead Derby in 1971. In an interview for *The Guardian* in August 2009, Harvey explained why: 'Basically, I had an argument with Douglas Bunn, the owner of Hickstead and one of the judges. I'd won the previous year and I was supposed to have brought back the trophy, but I left it at home. I said it didn't matter because I'd only win it again. He reckoned I couldn't. So I went and did it and when I did I turned to him and went: "Up yours."' It was a typically blunt response from a typically blunt Yorkshireman who failed to mention in that interview that Douglas Bunn took particular exception to the gesture and persuaded his fellow judges to disqualify Smith and have the prize of £2,000 removed. A massive row broke out and eventually both the Hickstead title and prize money were reinstated; some of the latter of which, Harvey gave away as a donation to the Riding for the Disabled Association.

## Still riding after all these years

Like Harvey Smith, Michael Whitaker began his riding life on a Shetland pony named Hercules whose main job was to pull a cart on a milk round. According to elder brother John: 'It was a proper old-fashioned milk float and Michael used to go out and catch the pony at six o'clock and by the time we got the harness on, got the milk which we'd loaded the night before and did the milk round, it was time for school.'

Things progressed in the intervening years and, on a combination of horses, the two brothers have won at least thirty-six Olympic, European and world medals between them. John competed many times on his horse Ryan's Son (well known to spectators as a result of his habit of swishing his tail while competing and then, after the last fence, putting in a buck!) and on Milton – said to have been the first horse outside of the racing world to have earned a million pounds.

Showjumping is in the Whitaker blood – the sons and daughters of both Michael and John are regular competitors and in 2024, John himself was still competing internationally at the highest level at the age of sixty-eight.

## Carrying a torch

Various equestrian disciplines have, of course, long been included in the Olympics and some of the riders competing have been involved in carrying the flame on its way to light the cauldron in whatever country the games might have been held that particular year.

The summer Olympics of 1956 were quite unusual in that, while the main event was held in Melbourne, Australia, all of the horse-related competitions actually took place in Stockholm, Sweden, due to very strict quarantine regulations set down by the Australian government. Not only were they held in a different country, but they also went ahead some five months prior to the main body of activities in Australia. As the flame headed through the Sweden and onto the capital, it was carried on its various stages by several equestrians and on arrival at the stadium, the cauldron was lit by dressage rider Hans Wikne.

On occasions when the flame was carried in relays through various parts of the UK, several British riders were involved. In 2004, eventer Pippa Funnell (three-time Olympic medallist and Rolex Grand Slam winner the previous year) was one of the torchbearers in the route through London riding a horse borrowed from the Household Cavalry. When the Olympics were held in London in 2012, some of the riders carrying the flame as it traversed around Britain included eventers Jane Holderness-Roddam, Zara Phillips (daughter of Anne, the Princess Royal who, during her own equestrian career, competed in the 1976 Olympics held in Montreal) and showjumping veteran, Harvey Smith.

More recently – and with typical Gallic flair and exuberance – when the flame was carried through France en route to the 2024 Olympic Games in Paris, one particular press agency reported that 'Fans went wild at the sight of the numerous champions amongst the … torchbearers [when] Pierre Durand, an Olympic gold medallist in the team jumping event at Seoul 1988, got the show on the road in Saint-Émillion …'

## Lost my bottle?

In 2024, Guy Simmonds, showjumper, rider and training coach, included the following on both his Instagram and Facebook pages – and has very kindly given permission to reproduce it here.

## A Clear Round

It contains much 'food for thought' together with some very wise words:

Someone recently opined that I'd 'lost my bottle'. It got me thinking ... have I? I think they were partially right, I will still get on most horses, and I'm certainly not scared, but I am more cautious. Does that mean I've lost my bottle?

I think as we get older we become more cautious in many ways of life, I myself don't bounce as well as I used to and recovery from injuries and hangovers takes a lot longer. I also think I've found better ways of training and curbing a horse's behaviour than jumping straight on and riding out whatever the issues are. I don't do things as I used to any more. I take more time and do a lot more homework. Whether it's evolution or just getting older and wiser I don't know but it's working – and if this means I spend less time eating sand, surely that's a good thing!

The flip side to this is that maybe I now have the luxury of not having to ride those type of horses. I get to be pickier about the horses I produce and am ultimately financially not in the position to have to take on any work and schooling liveries just in order to 'survive'.

I see it so often when I'm coaching clients; how many of them have lost confidence in their riding ability and in turn the horse has lost confidence in them. It's a vicious circle and a hard one to break free from. It seems that when we have children and responsibilities, we start to 'lose our bottle' as we come to the stark realisation that, if we get hurt, who's going to take on our responsibilities. The goal posts change – I suppose all we can do is try and ensure we follow a good code of practice and try and reduce the danger factor!

So, stop comparing yourself to what you used to be, how you used to ride and the horses you did ride – live in the present and be content with where you are now.

## Speak as you find

In certain quarters, there's a feeling (and some degree of evidence!) that showjumping (like hunting) encourages a degree of impropriety. Writing in 2007, the late and much-missed Clarissa Dickson Wright spoke of the horse world being full of 'genuine kindnesses, petulant resentments and energetic sexual encounters in the back of horseboxes'.

# 19

# DRESSAGE

Horse lovers, either actively involved or enjoying equine activities vicariously, give many reasons for their passion – and for their enjoyment of a particular discipline. The Rare Breeds Survival Trust (RBST) carried out a three-year project in which, in order to establish the versatility of native breeds, they asked owners and riders to identify the most frequent use to which they put their animals. Unsurprisingly, simple riding or hacking was the favoured activity with 75 per cent of respondents. Almost 53 per cent cited showing; 20 per cent showjumping – and almost 33 per cent undertook some form of dressage.

At its most basic, dressage is, as one exponent of the art describes it, 'all about working in harmony with your horse to help him improve suppleness, flexibility, obedience and athleticism – and ultimately become more pleasant and responsive to ride'. Elizabeth Letts, author of *Perfect Horse: The Daring U.S. Mission to Rescue the Priceless Stallions Kidnapped by the Nazis* maintains that dressage at its highest level 'demands more than skill; it engages a rider's inner wisdom and his ability to communicate with a mount in the silent language of horsemanship'.

In theory, almost any breed should, provided that they are blessed with reasonable conformation and the patience of a good trainer, be able to attain a basic standard. Nevertheless, in an article for *Horse & Hound* in October 2021, Polly Bryan mentions that 'the vast majority of horses [seen] competing successfully in top level dressage are warmbloods ... an athletic, modern type of horse ... such as the Dutch or Danish and German', the latter being 'one of many German horse breeds, including the Oldenburg, Westfalian, Hanoverian and Trakehner.'

## Whodunnit?

Some say that William Cavendish, first Duke of Newcastle (1503-1676) and a tutor of horsemanship to Prince Charles (later Charles II) brought the principles of dressage to England from Holland. Others say that King Henry VIII had been gifted four horses in 1514 from Francesco Gonzaga, an Italian nobleman in whose stables and riding arena, classical dressage was a regular discipline. Having taken a particular and very personal interest in these horses (described in Francesco Gonzaga's records of the time as being 'the flower of our stables'), Henry took intensive lessons with Italian riding instructors well versed in the art and, as often happens with such things, where royalty goes, others follow. If that's the case, dressage had then, obviously become popular some years before William Cavendish had any influence. That said, the duke is known to have been a brilliant horseman and was a great advocate of training horses through mutual understanding rather than breaking them through fear – about which he wrote two instructive manuals, the second of which (*A New Method to Dress Horses*, published in 1667) included comprehensive and somewhat revolutionary lessons in dressage.

*Dressage*

## Manège or ménage?

A manège (the word is French in origin) is an arena in which you can ride horses. They can be indoor or outdoor areas constructed for training, jumping, lunging, dressage and more – and tend to be covered with fillers such as silica sand or rubber chippings laid over a porous membrane. A ménage, on the other hand is a French word connected to a household or domestic situation.

It's surprising just how many times the latter word is misused when trying to describe the former – quite often by estate agents in their sales particulars appertaining to a country property with stabling, livery opportunities and other equine facilities.

## High kicks – and high school

The horses, riders and demonstrations of both the Spanish Riding School in Vienna and the National School of Riding in Saumur, France, continue to enthral both keen and knowledgeable horse people and tourists who simply enjoy the spectacle. They were, however, never intended as an attraction to bystanders and actually came into being as a way of training the cavalry in the fine arts of classical equitation. It's thought that the Spanish Riding School has been in existence since 1729, while what is now the National School of Riding in France was created as the Royal School of Cavalry in 1825.

Many of the 'moves' displayed by the horses and riders of the Spanish Riding School and France's National School of Riding are similar to some that might be seen during a display of dressage but were actually first developed as a means of instilling submission and manoeuvrability into a cavalry horse in training. The 'airs' above the ground are thought by some, to have been developed as a means of making a horse less likely to suffer injuries from the opposing sides in battle – for example, the 'capriole', whereby the horse leaps vertically in the air and kicks out with its hind legs at the same time. Others, however, say that they were never used during combat and were only ever intended to encourage response and make an animal quick to react when instructed to do so by its rider.

In France, the art or practice of advanced classical dressage in the Renaissance tradition is known as '*haute école*' while in Spain, the expression '*alta escuela*' describes an extension of classical dressage whereby the movements include piaffe, levade and other 'airs' above the ground. Both terms quite literally translate as 'high school'.

## Put your best foot forward

Fans of Jane Austen and other novelists of the time – and of films and television plays depicting the same era – may well be acquainted with the quadrille, a popular dance which was introduced to England from France around 1808. Few realise that the quadrille dressage sequence familiar to horse riders is named after the dance so loved by the aristocracy of Georgian England.

## Words of wisdom from the farrier's viewpoint

Jeremy Whaley has had a lifetime's involvement with horses – as both an owner and a farrier – and has kindly allowed me to include the following:

> As a farrier, when I look at a horse, my eyes are instantly drawn to the horse's feet. In the old days, it was not uncommon to look at them and think, 'Oh my god, who shod that?' Today, in this country [the UK], it is extremely rare to see horses' feet and think, 'I could do better than that'. When I see pictures of horses abroad that give a clear view of their feet, I frequently see poor, and sometimes positively criminal attempts at shoeing.

As I no longer work commercially, I think I can say without bias, that I'm not sure many horses owners truly appreciate the skill of their farriers, and not infrequently present their horses to be shod in inappropriate conditions – wet and or muddy legs, on unlevel and/or wet ground, in poor light, or exposed to bad weather. You have to remember these people are effectively surgeons who are there to help you get the best out of your horse.

A farrier's service is not just about putting shoes on your horse. From looking at your horse's feet and the way the shoes wear, he can give you good advice on how to keep those shoes on and promote good foot growth. Whilst some horses might be okay living out twenty-four/seven in fields in all weathers, others will have feet that will deteriorate in constant wet – these latter horses, a farrier can do very little to help, the problem lies with the wet, not the farrier.

Then I sometimes hear people complain about the price of shoeing – they hear the overall price and think that is the sum of money going into the farrier's pocket. It is not. The cost of materials, tools, cost and time of travelling between appointments has to be taken into consideration …

You can cut costs with many parts of keeping horses, but trying to cut costs with your farrier will usually end up with you paying more in the long run. 'No foot, no horse' – once you have learnt and understood that ancient idiom, you and your horse will enjoy equestrian life.

## Greenwich Mean Time – or farrier time?

Horse owners often need the farrier at the last minute – either because a shoe has been lost at a most inopportune moment just before a show, dressage test or similar event. Some owners, however, are a little tardy at anticipating when they should next book a visit from the farrier. In either situation, the availability (or not) of a farrier in such situations has often led to (usually good-natured) comment. Owners say things such as 'The farrier is coming out to us on Tuesday ... unfortunately he never tells us which Tuesday!' Farriers respond with 'A farrier is never late. They turn up exactly when they intended!'

## Watch out – there's a sponsor about
Timing is important – and exact timing crucial – in many equestrian disciplines. Rolex has long been associated with some of the most prestigious horse-orientated events both internationally (the Grand Slam of Show Jumping – considered to be the ultimate equestrian challenge with much money to be won) and nationally (they have been an Official Partner at the Royal Windsor Horse Show since 2016). The company's involvement in equestrianism has produced enviable partnerships with some of the world's finest riders and competitions in showjumping, eventing and dressage.

## What's she Werth?
German dressage rider Isabell Werth rode her horse Gigolo at every championship between 1992 and 2000 but at the Beijing Olympics she rode Satchmo with whom she won the team gold and the individual silver medals. Isabell and her dressage horses (which also include Weihegold Old and Bella Rose II) created partnerships which, according to many, have led her to become 'one of the most successful dressage riders in history'. Isabell's achievements make for impressive reading – she had, by 2021, won twelve Olympic medals. With her gold medal that year, Werth became only the third Olympian to win gold medals at six Olympic Games and, as of 2021, was also a nine-time world champion, a twenty-one-time European champion, plus winning fourteen individual national titles. Unsurprisingly, this remarkable

rider has been presented with Germany's highest sports award, the Silver Bay Leaf.

## Olympic qualifications

Equestrian sports first featured at the modern Olympic Games in 1900 but it was not until the games were held at Helsinki in 1952 that women took part in the dressage event for the first time – and dressage became a mixed-gender competition.

Ahead of the 2024 Olympics, British Equestrian (www.britishequestrian.org.uk) explained the fundamentals of dressage – and the rules applying to teams and competitors from qualifying nations:

> Dressage is a test of horse and rider's ability to perform a range of movements in harmony, across the gaits of walk, trot and canter. Seven judges mark the test from different points around the arena, which measures 60m x 20m. At an Olympic Games, qualified nations can put forward teams of three horse and rider combinations, plus one travelling reserve who can be substituted in at any point until two hours prior to the start of the team final following illness or injury to a team horse or rider. If a nation isn't able to qualify a team, they can put forward one individual horse and rider combination, subject to eligibility and qualification criteria.

## Golden oldie

At the age of fifty-seven, Carl Hester, MBE, was the oldest member of Team GB to compete in the 2024 Paris Olympics. Riding fourteen-year-old stallion Fame, it was the dressage rider's seventh Olympics; the second most by a British athlete: 'I've kind of got used to the "older Olympian" mantle ... [and] I can say it doesn't get easier as you get older, in fact it gets a lot worse ... The pressure is so different because once you've started winning then the pressure to keep winning is always there [but] I know how important it is for a sport that is lesser known that we keep winning.'

After having collected the full set of Olympic medals over a lifetime and coming sixth in the individual freestyle dressage held at Versailles during the 2024 games, Carl announced that he would not be competing at the 2028 Olympics scheduled to be held in Los Angeles. The Paris competition was, he said, 'the perfect way to go out … it was probably the best freestyle I've ever done. Why should I not retire after that?'

## Diversity and inclusion

In the summer of 2018, Wallace the Great became the first mule to enter (and win) a British dressage test. Originally rescued from Ireland (where he was, by all accounts, annoying local villagers by eating all their carefully tended flowers) by the Donkey Sanctuary at Sidmouth, Devon, Wallace was entered into the competition held in Gloucestershire by his rider Christie Mclean.

A mule is by definition, a hybrid born of a male donkey and a mare. Initially prevented from entering the event due to the fact that, under British dressage rules, no mules were allowed, media attention prior to the day helped persuade those at the top to change the criteria whereby only horses and ponies could become eligible. As a result of the changes, all animals born to a mare can now compete.

It was a test case worth pursuing as far as Christie was concerned due to the fact that eleven-year-old Wallace scored 67.6 per cent in the British Dressage Quest Club competition – and beat eight horses and ponies to take first place.

## Room for improvement

Seen on social media and ascribed to an unknown author, are five (tongue-in-cheek) signs that your dressage techniques might need some consideration:

1. Under judges' remarks the only comment is: 'nice plaits'.
2. Your 20-metre circle shape reminds the judge that she should buy eggs on her way home.
3. Sitting trot has caused some of your fillings to come loose.
4. Your horse believes 'free walk' means leaving the arena and heading towards the nearest patch of grass.
5. Impulsion is improved only after the horse sees monsters in the decorative conifers near letters marking the dressage arena.

## Figure it out

At times when things are not going as well as they ought to be in training, it might pay to keep in mind the words of Jeannette Walls, author of the book *Half Broke Horses* (Simon & Schuster, 2010): 'Horses were never wrong. They always did what they did for a reason, and it was up to you to figure it out.'

## Finely tuned

'Riding ... is like playing a finely tuned instrument, at times delicate, at other times powerful ... The true artist can play with equal dexterity a soft ballad or a crashing march.' So opines Sally Swift who is said to have developed the concept of Centered Riding – described as being 'an innovative way of expressing the classical principles of riding, using body awareness ... [and] encompasses all seats and styles of riding'.

## Gentleness and patience

Although having lived well over 2,000 years ago, Xenophon, a cavalryman, military general, scholar and friend of Socrates, in his book *The Art of Horsemanship* (one of the earliest-known references to horses and their well-being) includes much of relevance to today's equestrians – and a great deal of common sense. Take, for instance, this little snippet:

> ... when your horse shies at an object and is unwilling to go up to it, he should be shown that there is nothing fearful in it, least of all to a courageous horse like him; but if this should fail, touch the object yourself that seems so dreadful to him, and lead him up to it with gentleness. Compulsion and blows only inspire the more fear; for when horses are at all hurt at such a time, they think that what they shied at is the cause of the hurt.

## Mastering the art

From *Decorum: A Practical Treatise on Etiquette* (J. A. Ruth & Co., 1877): 'Never appear in public on horseback unless you have mastered the inelegancies attending a first appearance in the saddle.'

## No slouching or slovenliness

In 1838, an unknown scribe drew up a list containing eight pieces of advice for the lady equestrian. Number two on the list was this:

> Be easy, but not slovenly in the saddle. Nothing can be more detrimental to the grace of a lady's appearance on horseback, than a bad position, it is a sight that would spoil the finest landscape in the world. She ought to be correct, without seeming stiff or formal: and easy, without appearing slovenly.

## 20

# ANYONE FOR POLO?

With regards to the possible origins of the sport of polo, John Lloyd, author of *The Pimm's Book of Polo* (Stanley Paul, 1989) wrote:

> Where the game of polo was born will never be known – but written accounts tell of it being played by Iranian tribesmen some six hundred years before the birth of Christ. What is known, however, is that when Lieutenant Joseph Sherer – dubbed 'The Father of English Polo' in Calcutta in 1864 and who must be credited with the spread of the modern game – first came across it being played by local tribesmen at Silchar in the north-eastern Indian state of Manipur, he is said to have become excited and exclaimed 'We must learn this game!'

## Parental issues

The Hollywood actor Sylvester Stallone is often quoted as having once compared hitting a ball with a stick from horseback to being 'like trying to play golf during an earthquake'. Playing polo runs in the actor's family as his father Frank, was a professional polo player who competed in Italy before emigrating to New York in the 1940s. Stallone Jnr began playing polo aged eleven but a massive fall-out with his father (while actually on the polo field) meant that he didn't play again until in his forties. Sadly, according to a profile of the actor screened on *Netflix* in November 2023, another serious altercation with his father caused him to give up the game again – this time for good.

## It's all in the breeding

In her book *Horses and Ponies of Britain* (1944), Lady Wentworth tells her readers that

> Polo ponies are not a breed but a mixture of many breeds, Arabs, Thoroughbreds and Crossbreeds. The raising of the height limit from 14.2 [hands] has been a doubtful blessing as it admits a heavier type of pony which knocks out the lighter type and increases the cost of the game, making it a game for the few richer men, who can afford a long price, instead of a game within reach of many. It is in fact becoming semi-professionalised being more of a serious business than the sport it used to be.
>
> Before this alteration Arab polo ponies were pre-eminent for their cleverness, quickness and miraculous turning powers, just as they are pre-eminent in India for pig sticking, but now they have been ridden off the field by the sheer weight of the bigger ponies and with them go many young polo players whose purses cannot compete with the increased expenses.

Polo is certainly a serious and expensive business, and the cost of horses and the sport does indeed prevent participation by many. As a follower of the sport was once heard to say, 'Nothing is cheap in polo. The signs are always there, whether it is the preferred mode of transport to a game, the clothes worn or the lavishness of the post-game entertainment ... Horses, equipment and grooms all smell of money.'

*Anyone for Polo?*

## An empathetic partnership

In any equine discipline, but particularly polo, it is important to remember that, to be successful, there has to be empathy and understanding between pony and rider – and a great degree of dedication to the sport. Ralph Waldo Emerson, the nineteenth-century American essayist, once wrote that 'Riding a horse is not a gentle hobby, to be picked up and laid down like a game of solitaire. It is a grand passion.' More than a century later, Monty Roberts, the man known by many as the 'horse whisperer' opined: 'Horses are our silent partners. When we learn their language. This partnership grows strong.'

## Playing Ragtime

Sometimes two worlds – that of the battlefield of the First World War and the very different field on which polo is played – collide. That was certainly the case with Ragtime, a pony foaled in India in 1910 and ridden on both fields by Major Michael Willoughby.

Ragtime carried Willoughby for both military troop inspections and polo games, but the pair were separated when the major returned to India in 1916 – only to be reunited some twelve months later when Michael recognised his old mount during a polo event. The two then continued together for the remainder of the war and also took part in the Arab Revolt of 1920. Retired to Yorkshire, Ragtime 'wrote' and published his autobiography, *'Raggie' The Warhorse,* in 1931 – the proceeds from which were used to aid equine veterans of the First World War.

## Fit for purpose

Sometimes an equine intended for a particular use – in this instance, the parade-ground environment of a cavalry regiment –

might find his forte in another sphere. This extract from the April 1935 issue of *The Polo Monthly*, proves the point:

> The [horse] had, in fact, definitely shown that he had had a surfeit of this work by jibbing and kicking when asked to go into the enclosed school ... [and] had been warned off the parade ground by the Commanding Officer for kicking and biting ... he was probably the world's worst hack, but there was one thing he could do, and that was to play polo in his own way. He was one of those tragedies of life, a thoroughly misunderstood pony with a will and way of his own, an outlaw to most people, but a willing, brilliant performer to anyone who would let him play his own game. If left alone he would follow the ball like a terrier after a rat, and would come round like a flash of lightning when asked to do so, but entirely on his forehand and probably on the wrong leg. These little things did not matter to him so long as he got round quicker than other ponies, and a leg here or there made no difference whatever – but he never fell.

## Match fever

In 1937, Sidney Goldschmidt believed that some horses shared with their riders the peculiarity of 'match fever':

> It would not be wrong to say of a polo pony that the better bred he is the more highly strung he will be and the more susceptible to his surroundings. Nearly all ponies vary in what is required before the game, to bring them to a suitable frame of mind to play polo. Some of the more placid ones require nothing more than a walk, others a vigorous gallop up and down the ground with a strong pull up on their hocks a few times, others the few minutes with stick and ball that most players find necessary to 'get their eye in'.

## Go buy for me, Argentina

As well as those which are home-bred, a great many polo ponies playing tournaments in Britain, Europe and America originate either from New Zealand or, more usually, Argentina. There are some folk in the polo world who, early in the year, visit both countries seeking out suitable mounts for their clients and will, if you ask them, tell you that the easiest way for those clients to improve at polo is to invest in quality ponies.

Argentina in particular is well known for its quality of pony – usually thoroughbred or a mix of thoroughbred and Argentine criollo ('Polo Argentino') which, or so their breeders say, results in an agile, tough pony with a high resistance to injury. They are also said to be easier to handle and train. Training prior to sale can be a lengthy process as ponies generally only begin playing when they are around four years of age and their vendors prefer to let their horses have a couple of seasons on the polo field before selling an animal that will then hopefully have had sufficient 'play' time and experience to provide a near-perfect pony for their clients.

## It's a fact

A few facts about polo – garnered from the world of the internet and social media:

- During the Tang Dynasty (AD 618–709) 'Lvju' or donkey polo was a popular sport among Chinese women.
- While the sport of polo is known for being played from horseback (and, on occasion, donkeys!), it has, in some parts of the world, regularly been played from the backs of elephants, camels and even yaks.
- Popular with British soldiers serving in India, polo is said to have been initially referred to as 'hockey on horseback'.

- Founded in 1868, the Malta Polo Club is said to be the oldest polo club in the northern hemisphere – and the second oldest club in the world after the Calcutta Polo Club of India.
- Officers based at the barracks in Aldershot are reckoned to have organised the first-recorded game to be played in England at Hounslow Heath in 1869.
- The rule of players only being allowed to hold the mallet in their right hand was brought about for safety reasons after incidents where two horses approaching each other with riders holding their mallets in opposite hands resulted in head-on collisions or other injuries.
- Now a fashion item in some quarters, the traditional coloured belts worn by polo players, were first created when the gauchos (Argentine cowboys) were introduced to the sport and used colourful patterns (often diamond designs) as a way of helping to distinguish the competing teams.

## A sex problem

Possibly rather risqué for the time, in 1936, in *From Saddle and Fireside*, the author R. S. Summerhays titled one of the chapters 'A Sex Problem'. While it might have had adolescent schoolboys eagerly skipping through its pages, they would have been sadly disappointed as the problem referred to was one of whether or not females should play polo which, at the time, was almost exclusively male-dominated. After asking rhetorically, 'can the average woman stand up to polo ...?', it seems that Summerhays was very much in favour of females participating in the sport and pointed out that women 'are not only efficient riders, but exceptionally good ones' – and went on to opine:

Women too, have the advantage of men in their grace of carriage; and does not grace of carriage imply poise and balance, and are these not among the great essentials in riding, and particularly so in polo? Moreover, polo is a game of beauty surpassing all others in that respect, for, as properly played, all actual strokes, as distinct from pushing or hooking the ball out from a pony's legs, are things of dash and fire and of slashing curves synchronising and rhyming with every movement of the pony ...

Let all our riding women take some note of this and many will be found who, knowing that their entry to the game is encouraged rather than grudgingly tolerated, will enthuse that spirit of enthusiasm into the game for which it calls. A new field for women to conquer, a field where grace and beauty vitally abound, and where the spectacular is the commonplace.

In the ninety years since Summerhays wrote the above, the 'sex problem' has been significantly addressed and female players are very much on the scene – and competing in both women-only tournaments (with a separate league) and mixed polo. Clare Milford Haven remembers playing in one of the first women's polo tournaments at Cowdray Park during the late 1990s and is delighted to see, in the intervening years, just how many all-female tournaments there are both in the UK and around the world. Claire Tomlinson is another who first competed in what was then primarily a male-orientated sport and in the latter years, the likes of Rebecca Walters, Milly Hine, Hazel Jackson and Nina Clarkin have all become high-ranking UK players.

## Putting polo on the map

Several polo clubs in the UK have an illustrious history – but it is commonly thought that one of the most important is Cowdray Park, in Midhurst, West Sussex. Owned by the Pearson family – their inherited title being lord or viscount – it was in the immediate post-war years, that the third viscount did a great deal to put Cowdray Park on the polo map. A four-goal player in 1939, his lordship lost his left arm during the Second World War but, with the aid of a hook to hold the reins, continued to play until the 1960s. In *The Pimm's Book of Polo* John Lloyd mentions that, immediately after the war '... with the help of his stud groom, William Woodcock, he maintained an impressive string of fifty ponies [and] ... always generous and thoughtful, [he] was a great encourager of young players, lending his horses free to officer cadets from the Royal Military Academy at Sandhurst.'

## Prancing on ice

At the end of January each year, many of the great and the good of the polo world head towards the Swiss resort of St Moritz – but not, as one might imagine, for the ski slopes and the more traditional sport of skiing. Instead, their interest lies in the Snow Polo World Cup, a tournament played on the snow-covered ice of the lake situated in the Engadin Valley. It's an event first thought of in 1983 and the first-ever Snow Polo World Cup took place in 1985. Although (with the exception of the grandstand) entry to the event is free, it is very definitely not a place to go if you are on a budget. The sight of Cartier jewellery and watches (patrons, players and their teams compete for the Cartier Trophy) is as glittering as the snow on the lake and (Perrier-Jouët) champagne flows as freely as might a Swiss mountain stream in the springtime.

As to how the ponies manage to keep their footing when ridden on snow-covered ice, some wear special shoes which funnel the snow from the ball of their feet and help stop snow impaction. Studs provide extra grip and while in other instances where studs are employed and only a single one is screwed into the outside edge of the rear shoes, in snow polo studs are quite often fitted to both front and back shoes in order to gain better traction.

## Rather good exercise

Although generally considered a game for young, fit riders, polo had other enthusiast followers who thought it an excellent way of keeping active and healthy. In 1890, the future United States president Theodore Roosevelt wrote to a friend: 'I tell you a corpulent middle-aged literary man still finds a polo match rather good exercise.'

## Three of a kind

Mike Rutherford, of the band Genesis and also Mike and the Mechanics, was, for a quarter of a century, an accomplished and fanatical polo player. It is though, as he once said, 'a young man's sport' and admitted to having several mishaps while on the polo field: 'I've broken lots of bits ... my arm, my nose ... and knocked lots of teeth out.' Kenney Jones, one-time drummer with the Small Faces and The Who, was similarly enthusiastic about the game and when he bought a house and property near Cranleigh, Surrey, in the 1980s, created a polo pitch for his own amusement. The pitch was, however, soon developed and became the quite prestigious Hurtwood Park Polo Club attended by celebrities and several polo-playing members of the Royal Family. During the same period, Stewart Copeland, drummer of The Police, was just as keen on the game as his pop-star contemporaries and said of the sport, that it was 'much better than a drug habit'.

The three quite often got together to play charity matches and, as Mike Rutherford recalled during an interview for *Surrey Life* magazine in 2013, they very nearly had a team: 'There was myself, Kenney Jones [and] Stew Copeland ... and we took Roger Taylor [drummer of Queen] to a polo match ... thinking we might get him to be the fourth player.' Their plan did not, however, go quite as well as expected when 'in the first two or three minutes' of the game, someone fell off their pony right in front of the four of them and broke their arm – at which point, 'Roger decided that it wasn't for him after all ...'

## Bits and pieces

With any aspect of riding, there is a bewildering array of bridles and bits with which to furnish them. As well as those intended for general use, in the world of polo it is reckoned that the possibilities are even wider – and some seem quite sinister in name. There is, for instance, the Argentine Roller Mouth Pelham; the Hitchcock gag; the Balding or Half Moon gag; the French Bradoon and the Barry gag. The mind boggles!

## 21

# ALL THE FUN OF THE FAIR

In 1838, an unknown scribe gave their views on the desirability or otherwise of certain colours of horses – although in this instance, it was more to do with fashion:

> Of all colours presented by the horse, none is so rich, and, at the same time, so elegant and chaste, as a bright bay; providing the mane, tail and lower parts of the legs, be black. But much white, either on the face or legs, whatever be the general hue, is quite the reverse of desirable.

From the same unknown writer comes the advice that ladies (why only 'ladies' is not made clear) should not ride a horse which is anything less than perfect – and goes on to describe that which one should be looking for:

> The beau ideal of this kind of horse is superlatively elegant in form, exquisitely fine in coat, and unexceptionably beautiful in colour; of a height, in the nicest degree appropriate to the figure of the rider; graceful, accurate, well-united, and thoroughly safe in every pace; light as a feather in the hand, though not at all painfully sensitive to a proper action of the bit; bold in the extreme, yet superlatively

docile; free, in every respect, from what is technically denominated vice; excellent in temper, but still though gentle, yet not dull; rarely, if ever requiring the stimulus of the whip, yet submitting temperately to its occasional suggestions.

Some of these paragons of virtue were purchased from the stables of friends, from professional horse dealers and, on occasion, seasonal horse fairs.

## *Caveat emptor*

When considering purchasing a horse either through a dealer or at one of the many horse fairs dotted around the countryside, there was a great need for the would-be buyer to be careful that they weren't having 'the wool pulled over their eyes' or 'buying a pig in a poke' – both expressions in common usage in modern-day language and yet which have their origins in the animal trading fairs of old. Horse dealers would employ many 'tricks of the trade'; some quite benign such as standing a horse on slightly higher ground than the rest of the stable yard so as to make it appear taller. Other 'tricks' (numbing a bad foot with boiling turpentine, for instance) were infinitely cruel. In September 1911, *Country Life* warned its readers that, if considering buying a horse at a fair, it was prudent to take care:

> There was once a buyer who noted a particularly fine bay horse at the fair. He was told confidentially that the horse had been rejected on account of its hocks and – added the dealer candidly – 'I am none so sure of them myself.'
>
> The dealer thought he knew a curb when he saw it and could find nothing whatsoever the matter with what seemed to him a pair of unusually well-formed hocks. After a little chartering he bought the horse and sent him to his own stable. Next morning a friend

looked in and was taken proudly to see the new purchase, the story of which was told on the way to the stable. Directly the friend saw the horse he went straight up to his head and looked at him. Then, coming out of the stall, he cracked his hunting whip sharply behind the horse, which sprang forward and struck his head against the wall. The horse was stone blind, and the dealer's anxiety to draw attention to his hocks explained.

Author, poet, librettist, playwright and horse lover Ronald Duncan (arguably most famous for his poem *The Horse* – aka *An Ode to the Horse* – which has been read by various actors at the end of each Horse of The Year Show), described a visit to his West Country stable yard by a horse dealer in his 1953 book *Jan at the Blue Fox*:

> Both the man and his horse were well groomed with more spit than polish. The two-legged tyke wore gaiters, a Donegal tweed coat and cap of the same material. He looked prosperous without enough conscience to be ashamed of it. His horse, too, was spruce and shiny – but that didn't take me in. I knew the trick of brushing a horse over with a rag soaked in linseed oil to make it look in good condition.

## A fat body of men with their ruddy cheeks

Many venues for modern-day funfairs held around Britain were originally horse fairs, at which horses and ponies would be sold. One such, held each October, was at Wibsey, West Yorkshire – and was attended by horse traders from far and wide. They were, according to an account written in the very early days of the twentieth century: 'a fine, jolly, fat body of men, with their ruddy cheeks, smart appearance and jovial countenances'. History fails to mention whether the same could be said of those attending the likes of the Barnet Fair on the northern extremes of London in September; Broughton Horse Fair held each June near Northampton; Boroughbridge, North Yorkshire which, until the 1980s, was traditionally planned for the first Tuesday occurring after 22 June, and, of course, Widecombe Fair in Devon on the second Tuesday of September – which, as is well known due to the folk song of the same name, was attended by Tom Pearce's grey mare, Bill Brewer, Jan Stewer, Peter Gurney, Peter Davy, Dan Whiddon, Harry Hawke, Old Uncle Tom Cobley and all!

## No more, the Hayride

Despite the ever-dwindling numbers of horses working the land, many people continued to champion and celebrate the times when they were an essential part of everyday living both in the fields and in the towns. Although a festival rather than a fair, at Walkington in the East Riding of Yorkshire, there was, for several years, an event known as the Victorian Hayride held annually on the third Sunday of June. It was an occasion in which dozens of farm wagons, carts, traps and mounted riders travelled around the local villages, not only creating quite a spectacle, but also raising large sums of money for charity while doing so. According to some, it was reckoned to be the largest procession of horse-drawn wheels in England and was supported by the likes of Geoff Morton of Holme-on-Spalding-Moor. Geoff (and subsequently his two sons) were well known for farming with shire horses long after other farmers had taken to tractors and assorted farm machinery. Another stalwart was William (Bill) Cammidge from Flower Hill Farm at North Newbald who, in addition to being heavily involved in the Shire Horse Society, provided some of the horses which appeared in the original television series of *All Creatures Great and Small*.

Sadly, the Hayride is no more – it was discontinued after its 40th anniversary in 2007 when, in the words of Ernie Teal, one of the organisers quoted in the online *Walkington News* (https://www.walkington-news.org/what-was-hayride.html): 'We arrived back at Northlands Farm ... about six o'clock, bouquets verbal and flowery were given out, pies and peas were eaten; the horses fed and watered and yet another Hayride was over.'

## Appleby Horse Fair

Check your diaries for the date of the next Appleby Horse Fair which traditionally 'begins on the Thursday before the second Wednesday of June'. Assuming that the date can be identified by such seemingly and unnecessarily complicated mathematics, it is an event well known as a 'Gypsy, Roma and Traveller' (GRT) gathering and for the way they race their horses and ponies for sale (and for bets) up and down the local roads. Not only does it attract would-be vendors and purchasers, but it also creates a great deal of public interest and attention from reporters working for both local and national papers – many of whose photographers are keen to witness the washing of the animals for sale in the nearby River Eden. Quite often they are ridden bareback into the water by youngsters from the GRT community and so perhaps quite understandably, such images make a splash in many newspapers and on social media each year.

The spectacle is not, however, enjoyed by all. In recent times there have been attempts to ban the event because of apparent cruelty to some of the horses and ponies (nine animal welfare charities – all members of the National Equine Welfare Council – work together to support the protection and well-being of the horses at the event); apparent arrests for many and varied misdemeanours and excessive amount of litter strewn across the banks of the River Eden. A survey reported in the

*Cumberland and Westmorland Herald* in June 2023 claimed that local residents thought the event was 'unsafe and intimidating' and akin to the 'Wild West' while in 2024, *The News & Star* reported that a petition to prevent any future fairs from being held had been launched – in connection to which, a spokesperson for the Appleby Fair Communities Group went on record saying: 'The event we see today bears no resemblance to the event envisaged by Lord Lonsdale in 1911 when he gave Fair Hill to the town to be used for this event.'

## Horses from the Emerald Isle

Many horse fairs took place in Ireland and, especially when looking for a hunter, the Emerald Isle is where many would-be owners and horse dealers would once (and frequently still do) travel in the hope of buying suitable stock for would-be purchasers and clients. One of the reasons for doing so is that so many of the Irish horses (of varied breeding and backgrounds) had gained experience in the hunting field and, as a consequence, knew how to look after themselves. Showjumper Harvey Smith is said to have had a fondness for them for that very reason, believing that they thought for themselves and could get themselves out of trouble should the need arise. Others claim that once an Irish horse is taught something, it's never forgotten.

In 1870, 'The Druid', a noted writer on matters concerning farms, field sports and horses, wrote about the various mail coaches – and of the horses that pulled them. It seems that, at the time: 'Ireland furnished the greater portion of them, and they were picked up at Rosley Hill fairs. None under five years old were ever purchased, and the average of service in a fast mail was three years, although there were some brilliant exceptions. The worn-outs were sold back to farmers at £5 or £6, and mares, of course, commanded the best price.'

## Crowded carts and squealing colts

In *Some Experiences of an Irish R.M.*, by Somerville and Ross, published in 1899, Major Sinclair Yeates – who had recently obtained a position as Resident Magistrate (the 'R.M.' of the title) in rural Ireland – described his experience of being taken to a horse fair:

> As we neared the town of Drumcurran the fact that we were on our way to a horse fair became alarmingly apparent. It is impossible to imagine how we pursued an uninjured course through the companies of horsemen, the crowded carts, the squealing colts, the irresponsible led horses, and, most immutable of all obstacles, the groups of countrywomen ...
>
> It was eleven o'clock, and the fair was in full swing. Its vortex was in the centre of the field below us, where a low bank of sods and earth had been erected as a trial jump, with a yelling crowd of men and boys at either end ... Strings of reluctant horses were scourged over the bank by dozens of willing hands, while exhortation, cheers, and criticism were freely showered upon each performance.

## Suspicious minds

In the minds of many, the horse or pony pulling a traditional gypsy caravan ought to be either skewbald (brown and white) or piebald (black and white). It is often said that 'a good horse can never be a bad colour' yet the colour of a horse or pony has been the subject of whims of fashion – or even superstition – throughout the years. There is, for instance, this ancient adage, the reasoning behind which has always remained unclear:

> One white leg, buy him
> Two white legs, try him
> Three white legs, send him far away; sell him to your foes.
> Four white legs, keep him not a day; feed him to the crows.

## A grey area

In some quarters there is definitely prejudice regarding grey horses – but more for practical reasons rather than superstition. As those who own greys of whatever hue will be only too aware, Sod's Law will always have it that no matter how much care one takes in negating the possibility, on the morning of the day when it is imperative that your horse – prepared in readiness the day before – there is invariably a swear-inducing stain that occurred overnight which no amount of tomato ketchup (often said to be efficacious in removing stable and grass stains) or specifically manufactured products will ever totally eliminate in time for the event!

## First impressions

In 1933, author 'Spider' Jacobson advised his readers that, when looking to buy a new horse, first impressions are important: 'If you don't like the look of the horse to begin with, have no more to do with him; if you buy him you will probably hate the sight of him at the end of a month.'

## Bless you!

Buying a horse has often been considered to be more a matter of luck than judgement. On occasion, it might perhaps have required divine intervention to ensure that the horse was as described by either the dealer or in advertisements!

Throughout history, in certain areas of the countryside, there were traditions which involved the parish vicar blessing the local horses. In their book *Maypoles, Martyrs and Mayhem* authors Quentin Cooper and Paul Sullivan tell readers that 'St Ippollitts in Hertfordshire gets its name from St Hippolytus [a third-century horse doctor], whose relics are said to be buried at the local church and are said to have featured in the ceremony held there annually. On 13 August – the saint's feast day – sickly horses were led up to the altar and touched with one of his bones.'

A 'horseman's service' regularly took place at Scalby in North Yorkshire. After a short address by the local vicar, horses and their owners lined up at a makeshift altar by the village stream and each of the animals was given a blessing (and a handful of oats). Traditions die out and, for many years, the event at Scalby was thought to be one of only three such horseman's services held in England. It is interesting to note, however, that the blessing of animals – including horses, donkeys and ponies – seems to have undergone something of a revival in recent times.

In Central Park, Peterborough, the memorial to Jimmy the donkey (see Chapter 5, Equine Epitaphs) is visited regularly by schoolchildren, care home residents and members of the general public but, in February each year, on International War Animals' Day, a remembrance service is held at which a purple poppy wreath is laid and a minute's silence observed in honour of all animals lost in war – and to remember those affected by current conflicts. For over thirty years, Ely Cathedral has held an annual Animal Service to which people mainly bring dogs, cats, guinea pigs, rabbits, chickens – and the odd donkey and horse. Held inside the cathedral rather than out in the grounds, several animal charities nowadays benefit from the family-friendly/pet-friendly service and blessing. After a service held there in 2022, the *Cambridge Independent* newspaper reported that 'a very well-behaved horse called Thomas made a well-received appearance and a hungry donkey was spotted eating the order of service.'

22

# THE LAST LAUGH – A LITTLE ROUND-UP OF HORSE-RELATED JOKES

Sometimes, when things have not gone as well as one hoped, there's no alternative but to sit down on the horsebox ramp, an upturned wheelbarrow in the feed room or flop down on the bank of grass by the arena and smile – or better still, have an out-and-out laugh about things!

### Roadside assistance

Out in the countryside, a man accidentally drove his car into a deep ditch on the side of the road. Luckily a farmer happened by with his old horse Captain. The man asked for help and the farmer said Captain could easily pull his car out – and backed the horse up so as to be able to hitch him to the man's car bumper. Then he yelled, 'Pull, Nellie, pull.' Captain didn't move. Then he yelled, 'Come on, pull Duke.' Still Captain didn't move. Then he shouted really loudly, 'Now pull, Blossom, pull hard.' Captain just stood. Then the farmer nonchalantly said, 'Okay, Captain, pull,' – and, with ease, the horse pulled the car out of the ditch. The driver was obviously very appreciative but naturally curious and asked the farmer why he called his horse by the wrong name three times – to which the farmer replied, 'Oh, Captain is blind and if he thought he was the only one pulling he wouldn't even try.'

## Artwork
Yesterday I saw a horse-drawn carriage – the proportions were a bit off, but the shading and line-work were quite remarkable.

## Why?
If you're not supposed to put the cart before the horse, why is it called a carthorse?

## A question of mathematics
A horse walks into a bar and says to the barman, 'On a right-angled triangle with sides x, y and z, if x and z are perpendicular, which side is opposite the right angle?' And the barman replies, 'Y, the long face.'

## Something for everyone
A sign seen at a riding stables proclaimed:

> For fast riders, we have fast horses.
> For slow riders, we have slow horses.
> For those who have never ridden before, we have horses that have never been ridden.

## You love that horse more than you love me
Jane's husband was complaining again: 'You care more for your horses than for me, I bet that you can't even remember when we got married!'

'Of course I can, darling,' replied Jane, 'it was the day after I won my first-ever dressage test!'

## Seeing sense

A man left for work one Friday morning – but went to the races in the afternoon. Meeting up with friends, he went on with them to celebrate several wins on the horses. Staying out all night, he then went racing again on the Saturday. When he finally arrived home, he was confronted by one very angry wife.

'How would you like it if you didn't see me for two or three days?' she said and he, equally angry, replied 'That would be fine with me.'

Monday went by and he didn't see his wife. Tuesday and Wednesday came and went with the same results.

On Thursday, the swelling had gone down just enough for him to see her a little out of the corner of his left eye.

## A tall story

A man was complaining that he couldn't tell his two horses apart from each other. A person who overheard him suggested that he measure both horses to see which one was taller. This wouldn't help him at all, he said, because the brown horse was the same size as the white one.

## Jobseeker's allowance

A horse walks into a pub and orders a pint of beer together with a cheese and lettuce sandwich. The barman looks at him and says, 'Hang on! You're a horse.'

'I see your eyes are working,' replies the horse.

'And you can talk!' exclaims the barman.

'I see your ears are working, too,' says the horse. 'Now, if you don't mind, can I have my beer and my sandwich please?'

'Certainly, sorry about that,' says the barman as he pulls a pint for the horse. 'It's just we don't get many horses in this pub. What are you doing around this way?'

## The Last Laugh – A Little Round-up of Horse-related Jokes

'I'm working on the building site across the road,' explains the horse, 'I'm a plasterer.'

The flabbergasted barman cannot believe the horse and wants to learn more but takes the hint when the horse pulls out a newspaper from his bag and proceeds to read it. So, the horse reads his paper, drinks his beer, eats his sandwich, bids the barman good day and leaves.

The same thing happens for two weeks. Then one day the circus comes to town. The ringmaster comes into the pub for a pint and the barman says to him, 'You're with the circus, aren't you? Well, I know this horse that could be just brilliant in your circus. He talks, drinks beer, eats sandwiches, reads the newspaper and everything!'

'Sounds marvellous,' says the ringmaster, handing over his business card. 'Get him to give me a call.'

So, the next day when the horse comes into the pub the barman says, 'Hey, Mr Horse, I reckon I can line you up with a top job, paying really good money.'

'I'm always looking for the next job,' says the horse, 'where is it?'

'At the circus,' says the barman.

'The circus?' repeats the horse.

'That's right,' replies the barman.

'The circus?' the horse asks again. 'With the big tent?'

'Yeah,' the barman replies.

'With all the animals who live in cages, and performers who live in caravans?' says the horse.

'Of course,' the barman replies.

'And the tent has canvas sides and a big canvas roof with a hole in the middle?' persists the horse.

'That's right!' says the barman.

The horse shakes his head in amazement and says, 'What on earth would they want with a plasterer?'

## Quackers
Q: What's the difference between a horse and a duck?
A: One goes quick and the other goes quack.

## A detailed defence
The teacher asked her pupils to make a sentence using the words 'defence', 'defeat' and 'detail' – at which, one little boy eagerly raised his hand and shouted out: 'When a horse jumps over defence, defeat go first then detail ...'

## Goodbye, Gordon
Although supposedly a true anecdote rather than a joke – and appertaining to a camel rather than a horse, I nevertheless found this story too amusing not to include:

> A British civil servant stationed in Egypt had a small son who showed a touching attachment to a local statue of General Gordon mounted on a camel. Every day the boy would visit Gordon's statue, staring admiringly upward. As they prepared to return to England, the boy begged for a farewell visit to the statue. 'Goodbye, Gordon,' he sobbed. The father was quite moved by this display of patriotism. Then, as they turned away, the boy suddenly thought to ask: 'Daddy – who's that man on Gordon?'

## Carburettor trouble
A man's car breaks down on a country road. When he gets out to fix it, a horse in the nearby field comes up alongside the fence and leans over by him. 'Your trouble is probably in the carburettor,' says the horse. Startled, the man jumps back and runs down the road until he meets a farmer. He tells the farmer his story.

*The Last Laugh – A Little Round-up of Horse-related Jokes*

'Was it a large white horse with a black mark over the right eye?' asks the farmer.

'Yes, yes,' the man replies.

'Oh, I wouldn't listen to her,' says the farmer, 'she doesn't know anything about cars.'

## Q & A

Q: When is a horse not a horse?
A: When it is turned into a paddock.

Q: Why did the owner name his racehorse Bad News?
A: Because bad news travels fast.

Q: How can you tell a police horse from a normal horse?
A: The police horse goes, 'Neigh-naw-neigh-naw-neigh-naw.'

## Out on the tiles

I had to leave my job at the ceramics factory when they introduced the new equestrian range ... it was turning into a horse tile work environment.

## Keep on trucking

Many horse owners use a Land Rover (other four-wheel drive vehicles are available!) to tow their horse trailers – with mixed results.

They say 90 per cent of all Land Rovers manufactured are still on the road – the other 10 per cent have reached their destination.

## Riding Rules for the Middle-aged Horsewoman

Finally, the following are some light-hearted 'rules' taken from a much longer list compiled by an 'unknown author'. There is no sexism intended in the title – which is included here just as it was written!

- Moaning, groaning and complaining about aching muscles is perfectly acceptable, as is taking Motrin (or something stronger) prior to a ride.
- Mentioning that it is too hot, too dry, too humid, too cold, too wet, etc., is considered self-expression, not whining.
- We will take time to discuss the important issues of the day, like who is dating who, who is cheating on who and any other relevant information that needs to be passed on.
- Helping someone on or off the horse does not mean the rider is an invalid. It only means the horse got taller overnight.
- We acknowledge that horses are very strange animals and that sometimes, for no reason at all, we fall off them. If this happens to any rider, the other riders will ascertain that the person is okay and then not mention the incident to another living soul, especially significant others.
- We need to keep this riding thing mysterious and strange sounding. If everyone finds out how much fun it is, the price of horses will go up and we will not be able to afford a dozen of them.

# BIBLIOGRAPHY, REFERENCES AND SOURCES

Alexander, Karen (editor), *The Changing Year* (Harmsworth Active, 1993).
Archer, Fred, *Hay Days: Memories of Country Life in the 1920s* (Sutton Publishing, 2001).
Astley, Sir John Dugdale, *Fifty Years of My Life*, Vol. II (Hurst and Blackett, Ltd, 1894).
Billett, Michael, *A History of English Country Sports* (Robert Hale Ltd, 1994).
Bryant, Mark, *Casanova's Parrot and Other Tales of the Famous and Their Pets* (Ebury Press, 2002).
Buckton, Henry, *Yesterday's Country Village* (David & Charles, 2005).
Carter, Sam (ed.), *Curious Observations: A Country Miscellany* (Simon & Schuster UK Ltd, 2011).
Coates, Rosemary, *Horse Riding Terms: An Illustrated Guide* (Merlin Unwin Books, 2018).
Cobbett, William, *Rural Rides* (The Political Register, 1830).
Cooper, Jilly, *Animals in War* (Corgi, 1984).
Cooper, Quentin and Sullivan, Paul, *Maypoles, Martyrs and Mayhem* (Bloomsbury Publishing, 1994).

Cope, Alfred, *Cope's Royal Cavalcade of the Turf* (Cope's Publications Ltd, 1953).

Dickson Wright, Clarissa, *Spilling the Beans* (Hodder & Stoughton, 2007).

Duncan, Ronald, *Jan at the Blue Fox* (The Country Book Club, 1953).

Edinburgh, HRH the Duke of, *Thirty Years On and Off the Box Seat* (J. A. Allen & Co. Ltd, 2004).

Evans, George Ewart, *Horse Power and Magic* (Faber & Faber, 1979).

Forrest, Susanna, *The Age of The Horse: An Equine Journey through Human History* (Atlantic Books, 2016).

Goldschmidt, Lt-Col Sidney G., *Skilled Horsemanship* (Country Life Ltd, 1937).

Gordon, W. J., *The Horse World of London* (The Religious Tract Society, 1893).

Hamilton, Jill, *Marengo: The Myth of Napoleon's Horse* (Fourth Estate, 2000).

Henry, Marguerite, *Misty of Chincoteague* (Rand MacNally & Co., 1947).

Hick, Frank L., *Ploughman's Kid* (Maxiprint, 1994).

Hilder, Rowland, *Horse Play: A Necessary Book on the Lighter Side of Riding* (Golden Galley Press, 1945).

Hobson, Jeremy, *Curious Country Customs* (David & Charles Ltd, 2007).

Holt, Peter, *The Keen Countryman's Miscellany* (Quiller Publishing, 2012).

Holt, Peter, *The Keen Foxhunter's Miscellany* (Quiller Publishing, 2010).

Ingrams, Richard, *Cobbett's Country Book: An Anthology of William Cobbett's Writings on Country Matters* (David & Charles/Reader's Union, 1975).

Jack, Albert, *Red Herrings and White Elephants* (Metro Publishing, 2007).
Jacobson, 'Spider', *Horses from Dealer to Covert* (Constable & Co. Ltd, 1933).
Lambton, Lucinda, *Palaces for Pigs: Animal Architecture and Other Beastly Buildings* (English Heritage, 2011).
Letts, Elizabeth, *Perfect Horse: The Daring U.S. Mission to Rescue the Priceless Stallions Kidnapped by the Nazis* (Ballantine Books, 2017).
Lloyd, John, *The Pimm's Book of Polo* (Stanley Paul & Co. Ltd, 1989).
Looker, Samuel J. (ed.), *The Chase: An Anthology for Huntsmen* (Daniel O'Connor, 1922).
Loriston-Clarke, Jennie, *The Complete Guide to Dressage* (Stanley Paul & Co. Ltd, 1987).
Lyon, Lt-Col W. E. (ed.), *The Horseman's Year 1946–1947* (Collins, 1947).
Mackenzie, Captain Cortlandt Gordon, *Notes for Hunting-Men* (Longmans, Green & Co., 1902).
Madol, Hans Roger, *The Private Life of Queen Alexandra: As Viewed by Her Friends* (Hutchinson & Co. Ltd, 1940).
May, Chris, *The Horse Care Manual* (Stanley Paul & Co. Ltd, 1987).
Mitchell, W. R., *The John Peel Story* (Dalesman Publishing Co. Ltd, 1968).
Mitchum, Petrine Day, (with Pavia, Audrey), *Hollywood Hoofbeats: The Fascinating Story of Horses in Movies and Television* (Companion House Books, 2014).
Moore, Tim, *Spanish Steps: Travels With My Donkey* (Jonathan Cape, 2004).
Morgan, W. A. (ed.), *The House on Sport* (Gale & Polden Ltd, 1899).

Porter, Val, *Milland: Living Memories* (Milland Memories Group, 2003).
Rees, Lucy, *The Horse's Mind* (Hutchinson, 1984).
Ross, Alan (ed.), *What are U?* (André Deutsch Ltd, 1969).
Seely, General Jack, (with an introduction by Brough Scott), *Warrior: The Amazing Story of A Real War Horse* (Racing Post Books, 2011).
Sewell, Anna, *Black Beauty: The Autobiography of a Horse* (first published by Jarrold & Sons, 1877).
Smith, Horace, *A Horseman Through Six Reigns – The Reminiscences Of A Royal Riding Master* (Odhams Press Ltd, 1955).
Summerhays, R. S., *From Saddle and Fireside* (Country Life Ltd, 1936).
Thelwell, Norman, *Wrestling with a Pencil: The Life of a Freelance Artist* (Methuen Publishing Ltd, 1986).
Timbs, John, *Curiosities of London: Exhibiting the Most Rare and Remarkable Objects of Interest in the Metropolis; With Nearly Fifty Years' Personal Recollections* (David Brogue, 1855).
Vesey-Fitzgerald, Brian, *Portrait of the New Forest* (Robert Hale & Company, 1966).
Waistell, Charles, *Designs for Agricultural Buildings* (Longman, Orme, Brown, and Green, 1827).
Welcome, John, and Collens, Rupert, *Snaffles: The Life and Work of Charlie Johnson Payne 1884–1967* (Stanley Paul & Co. Ltd, 1987).
Wentworth, Lady Judith, *Horses and Ponies of Britain* (William Collins Sons & Co., 1944).
Willett, Peter, *The Thoroughbred* (Weidenfeld & Nicolson, 1970).
Woodyard, Chris, *The Victorian Book of the Dead* (Kestrel Publications, 2014).

*Bibliography, References and Sources*

Woollett, Lisa, *Rag and Bone: A Family History of What We've Thrown Away* (John Murray, 2020).

Xenophon (translated by Morgan, Morris H.), *The Art of Horsemanship* (Dover Publishing, 2006).